# MOTHERING WITH SOUL

## Raising children as special work

### *Joan Salter*

Hawthorn Press

Published by Hawthorn Press,
Hawthorn House, 1 Lansdown Lane, Stroud, Gloucestershire, GL5 1BJ
Tel. (01453) 757040    Fax. (01453) 751138

Edited by Matthew Barton
Typeset at Hawthorn Press by Frances Fineran
Printed by Redwood Books, Trowbridge, Wiltshire
Cover design by Ivon Oates

Grateful acknowledgements to Sue Schuster for her drawings.

A catalogue record of this book is available from the British Library Cataloguing in Publication Data

ISBN 1 869 890 84 1

# Contents

## ACKNOWLEDGEMENTS

So many people have contributed to this book that I find it impossible to name them all. I therefore offer my sincere gratitude collectively.

There are only two special 'thankyous' I can mention – first to Dr Michaela Glöckler, paediatrician and leader of the Medical Section of the School of Spiritual Science (anthroposophy) at the Goetheanum, Switzerland. I feel greatly indebted to her for writing a foreword, and wish to record my gratitude.

Secondly, the book only became possible because of all the special mothers who have attended the Gabriel Baby Centre over the last 20 years. It is from them that I have learnt about mothering, and for this I wish to say a special 'thankyou'. To those who have written of their experiences (expecting, birthing and mothering) I am immensely grateful.

Joan Salter

# Foreword

*by Michaela Glöckler*

*The Incarnating Child* by Joan Salter made readers throughout the English-speaking world, not only in Australia, aware of the fact that there is life before birth. There is life in the world of the spirit out of which the decision is made to incarnate, look for particular parents and select a particular set of genes. Incarnation is a dramatic process, for the child has to come to terms with the genetic material inherited from its parents and also adapt to a particular part of the world, a particular historical period and highly individual family and school situations.

In her new book, *Mothering with Soul,* readers will see a different side of the author, a deeply committed educationalist and adviser. They will meet a woman who takes motherhood very seriously indeed, presenting everything essential for the care and nurturing of children, above all in early infancy, and at the same time also looking for and illuminating the spiritual roots of motherhood. The image she creates of our humanity – as mother, father and child – is good to have at a time when the role of the mother is widely rejected, to the point where parenthood is reduced to the level of mere partnership. While feminists laud female qualities, female archetypes, social structures and spirituality to the skies, Joan Salter has succeeded in presenting the solemn dignity of motherhood and also in showing that to be a mother is one of the most **important vocations in this century,** though this is not recognised in economic terms by any country on earth nor by any social system. This makes it a revolutionary book. If it were to be taken seriously, tax funds would have to be redistributed on a major scale to provide salaries for mothers, who provide the basis for society and state. Bringing up their children well they make it possible to save financial resources that otherwise have to be spent to deal with the consequences of not having achieved this primary socialisation. To be wholly dedicated to the existence and development of another human being, helping him to find and understand his life's mission for the benefit of the community, is a cultural achievement that makes more of a contribution to the common weal than many international congresses on social issues. I would therefore like to thank Joan Salter on behalf of the countless mothers whose work is not given the moral or material recognition it deserves. Her voice is an important contribution to truly valuing the mission and significance of motherhood, something that is urgently needed for our present time and the immediate future.

Michaela Glöckler

Medical Section at the Goetheanum
Dornach, Switzerland
Autumn of 1996

# Introduction

Let me begin by saying that this is not a book about 'feminism', nor about masculine-feminine issues (sexism) as they are often discussed today. I have written the book because I am convinced that good-quality mothering is central to the wellbeing of children, to the whole family, and in consequence to all contemporary humanity.

Hundreds of books on all aspects of child-care and parenting exist today. But this multiplicity of ideas and approaches also represents something of a maze in which the specific work of the full-time mother easily gets lost. Very often (in fact, usually!) it is undervalued and regarded as dull – so much so that many young women feel they need almost apologise for making mothering a full-time vocation. To correct this viewpoint and search for a deeper, broader view of a mother's tasks, is of urgent necessity today if family life is to be preserved. A mother's work needs to be recognized as pivotal to a healthy society.

This book attempts to elaborate on this point of view, to portray the essential nature of mothering and show what it can mean for women today. It does not try to resurrect an unreal or fanciful picture based on nostalgia for a by-gone age, but starts from the experiences and thoughts of young mothers at the present time. This book has grown from conversations I have had with hundreds of young women, my own observations of the human scene, and the spiritual scientific knowledge of Rudolf Steiner.[1]

Mothering and parenting are two essential but *different* activities. Parenting is an activity shared between two adults, usually father and mother, and involves nurturing, caring, guiding and undertaking many practical activities. It occurs on a soul and physical level, and as such contributes a great deal to the child's inner growth and practical upbringing.

Mothering, on the other hand, is essentially a spiritual activity, a woman's intimate connection with her child – one that only a mother can have. It is a career of the heart. Mothering starts from the very beginning of pregnancy, when a woman shares her body with her child, building the infant's body from her own substance. She then experiences the intensity of birth, again gives freely of her own body substance in the breast milk, and for the first three years of the child's life enfolds the little one within the forces of her own soul.[2]

As this book will attempt to show, mothering therefore makes possible an awakening of strong heart forces – which are today in danger of becoming dormant as our material way of life rides roughshod over essentially human qualities. Mothering nourishes the feeling life, enhances and releases qualities that can be described as spiritual – such as joyfulness, tenderness, patience and so on, which may otherwise remain deep within the soul, buried and unused.

For the mother herself this is an experience which no other calling in life, no daily occupation or profession (however intellectually stimulating), can even faintly match; for mothering, more than anything else, gives an opportunity to enhance the feminine qualities mentioned above. It demands a kind of **thinking** imbued with creative imagination, similar to a fairy story's magic spell; a **feeling** life capable of sacrificial love; and a strength of **will** born of the need for decisive action to steer a clear course through the hurly-burly of daily home life. It is a total soul involvement, connecting both mother and children with profound realities of spirit.

It will therefore be recognized that mothering is a unique womanly art of the very highest order. Such recognition in no way undermines the contribution of father, nor does it deny an art of parenting that is right for our times. Mothering brings its own unique contribution to life, enriching it and offering untold treasures of the human heart.

This book has been written in homage to my many young friends who make mothering a vocation.

# Prologue

## The Child speaks:

*Dear Mother,*

*I was an old, old man. Many times had I journeyed through the stars, garnering much fruit, preparing the next stage of life. I have travelled far, awaiting your call. In the Saturn sphere I heard the great clock chime the cosmic midnight hour, and knew the time had come.[1] Then into your body the seed was planted and received by your loving heart. Soon afterwards I entered. You expected me, for we had been in connection with each other. Within your warming, encompassing body, my own body grew. It was tended throughout by celestial beings including the sublime Madonna herself.[2]*

*My whole being was nurtured and prepared. You had given me a female body.*

*I strongly sensed father's presence as birthing began. We were all elated. It was a fire experience, initiating us into higher realms of awareness. I heard your singing as I came into the world.[3] It was as though the angels sang.*

*Thankyou dear mother for your bounteous gifts.*

## The Virgin Mother speaks:

*I am the Virgin Mother, the universal Divine Feminine, the archetypal Mother-being. I bring love and tenderness to earthly beings. I have been with you since primordial times, and you have known me as Isis, Artemis, Demeter and Diana. I can now reveal myself to you again if you will open wide the door of your heart. Then I will enter and fill your heart with my divine joy. I am the feminine love of the mother.*

*The Divine Sophia will bring you wisdom to weave into your heart. Her radiant light warms and illumines. Together we will inspire the angels working within your body, tending the child. [4] Open your heart to me and then I will be able to sustain you when your hour is come.*

*I will be with you, pouring strength into your heart, enfolding you within
my mighty aura, weaving my cloak around you.*

*I will always be with you in your mothering, for I also have mothered
a child. I have danced the dance of ecstasy, wept the tears of despair,
sobbed the desperate sob, and laughed the laughter of merriment. I am
the Virgin Mother. I salute and bless you, human mother.*

## The Father speaks:

*Dearest Ones,*
*The seed was planted strong and deep. It germinated, for the soil had
been carefully prepared. Reverence, tenderness and wonder, the
fertilizers of the soul, allowed the spark to penetrate, and ignite. Love
nourished the seed. The mingling of our auras expressed itself in radiant,
delicate colour.*

*Was it a moment or eternity?*

## The Mother Speaks:

*My darling Child,*
*As you suckle at my breast, I see only your innocent beauty. You smile,
and my heart thrills at your greeting. I offer you my body, I enfold you
with my love, and my spirit asks the help of heaven as I envisage your
life ahead. I seek your true being, but for the present it is hidden. Later
we will know each other face to face. My child, let us accept the past,
value the present, and seek in the future a meeting in spirit, in love and
in freedom.*

*I greet you, my companion of lives.*

## Again the Child speaks:

*Dear Parents,*
*Know me! I live in this engaging small body, and my soul is pure. You
are entranced with my beauty and innocence. Yet, my past awaits me
deep within my soul. Only at puberty will it be released. It holds a
multitude of secrets, extending over countless diverse lives.*[5]

*I have known the Waste Land, travelled in the desert of the soul. And* the towering sharp pointed rocks that block the way upward to the mountain top, these also have I known.

I have worshipped in the temple of Isis, begged solace of the great Mother at Ephesus, drunk deep from the wineskins of Bacchus, driven Caesar's chariot and slain with bloodied sword. I have heard tell of the New Way in Galatia – Oh, foolish Galatians! What error, what blasphemy!

There have been the lush forests of life, and I have tasted their honey and spices. I have seen the wild bees in their frenzied swarming, observed the many-hued beetle and the industrious ant. It was the ant which inspired me, brought me back to the plain of meaning, to the industry of life.

I have no regrets for past experiences, nor for the lush forests. They have all been part of the journey of lives. Isis taught me, Artemis fed me, Bacchus befogged me, Caesar drove me, and the New Way saved my soul. In the lush forests I learnt of life's thorns, its seductive vines, voluptuous scents, secret wells and hidden paths. I have wandered far into the forests and tasted their compelling sweetness.

Dear Mother, forgive me. Dear Father, accept me.

## The Parents speak:

Dearest Child,
We also have been there. Come, let us journey on....

# PART 1

# MOTHER

# 1
# Expecting

*Beloved Child, I greet you*

In the beginning was Love; and with love the cell was fertilized; and on the seventeenth day the spirit entered. It was an auspicious beginning.

The primordial substance was creative love. It is perceivable through the heart, and mothers **know** it; they live within it, experiencing it deeply. Thus expecting begins, and mothering too, for mothering commences at conception.

With love an expectant mother embarks upon a journey, one involving her whole being of body, soul and spirit. It is a journey which encompasses both her inner and outer life. Physiological and hormonal changes occur in her body, feelings intensify in her soul. She senses the spirit working within her, and connects to its light and strength.

For many mothers today – those sensitive to life's more subtle nuances – pregnancy opens gates to the spirit. In olden days people quite naturally spoke of 'heaven', and knew its 'inhabitants' as angels, archangels and so on. Today we have largely lost this pictorial imagery and tend to scoff at such things. But during pregnancy, women are increasingly entering into real contact with a non-earthly dimension of life and are willing to speak about such experiences.

To fully understand the processes taking place within her body, the mother-to-be needs an accurate picture of what the human being is. The one who has taken up abode within her uterus is a threefold entity: the embryo/foetus composed of living substance; the soul life ('the unborn child is an aware reacting human being, who, from the sixth month on ... leads an active emotional life');[1] and the human spirit (ego) seeking a further life on earth. According to spiritual scientific research, processes within the uterus are guided from the beginning by beings of spirit. Rudolf Steiner, in a lecture given in October 1917, had this to say:

> You should never believe that human birth and death are actually as they present themselves to the senses. Spiritual entities are involved when a human being enters the physical world from the non-physical.[2]

Geoffrey Hodson[3] has outlined in some detail the work of these 'spiritual entities' as they tend the growth and development of the physical embryo and the subtle bodies. He further describes how, in the eighth month, these beings are penetrated by what he calls 'the feminine principle in divinity'. In the Prologue this Being is called 'The Virgin Mother'. Hodson, from his own spiritual research, describes her as 'radiant and beautiful beyond description [...] The glory of divinity is all about her.' It is this sublime being who guides the human spirit to earth, to enter into a further incarnation. Knowledge of this, of these deeper aspects of 'expecting', prepares the soul of the mother-to-be for her special vocation of mothering, and helps her to fulfil her special task.

We will now hear what four young women experienced during pregnancy.

## Nora and the visitation

Nora (not her real name) was eight months pregnant, expecting her first child. She was Australian, and her husband Fijian. Nora had lived in Fiji for several years, steeping herself in the traditional culture of the people. She and her husband had come to Australia to have the baby. They were sitting at opposite sides of the kitchen table when Nora became aware of an infant (a girl) sitting on her husband's knee, facing outward, smiling at her. The 'vision' lasted momentarily. After the birth, her baby daughter looked exactly like the child she had seen earlier. The father had not been aware of this – the being of the child had revealed itself to the mother only.

# Dorothy and the Seal

About six months before her marriage to Gordon, a man of Scottish descent, Dorothy began to dream about the Scottish highlands, and often found herself singing Scottish songs. She had always been vaguely aware of her connection to Celtic myth, and after her marriage this was greatly accentuated. She had a strong feeling within the depths of her soul that these ancient Celtic people and their mythological life were part of her. She herself had Scottish blood and ancestry.

Kyle was her second child, and during her pregnancy these feelings and thoughts were strong within her.

A few weeks after Kyle's birth, Dorothy participated in the group singing of an ancient Celtic myth from the Orkney Islands. This was a heart-rending lament for the people's loss of ancient psychic vision. It was an experience that penetrated right into Dorothy's heart. She felt as though the wisdom of the Celts – their ancient rituals and knowledge of mankind's origin – entered into her, filling her soul and deeply affecting her.

At seven and a half months Kyle began to crawl. Perhaps it was not surprising that he did so in a special way – making a seal gesture! – for ancient people from the Orkney Islands believed that in the beginning of all things their human ancestors had been half seal.

There are many myths surrounding seals. Dr Karl König, the eminent Austrian embryologist, describes them as 'our brothers'.[4] Ancient myths tell how the Eskimos once lived in close connection with seals, and Dr Franz Boas says, 'the mother of the sea mammals may be considered to be the chief deity of the Central Esquimaux. She is supposed to bear supreme sway over the destinies of mankind.'[5]

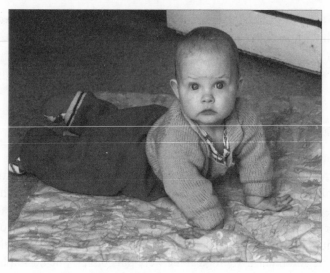

*Kyle makes a seal gesture*

König concludes his treatise on seals by quoting the Lapp Aslak (1944):

> Aslak, son of Siri Matti, told of the seals' origin 'as the fathers have handed (it) down' [...and] added this comment: 'If you pay attention when you take the skin off a seal, it looks almost like a man.' We could add to this the comment of a Labrador seal trader, Lambert de Boilleau (1850) – 'there is such a human expressiveness in their eye, in fact, in their entire visage'.[6]

As Kyle developed it became increasingly obvious that he was very different from his older brother, Kieran. The latter could be described as 'outward' in his orientation to life. He is fascinated by money matters (e.g. how much things cost), and other down-to-earth things, whereas Kyle is more inwardly focused, able to concentrate for longer periods, fascinated by stories etc. He is also fascinated by water, and as a small child loved to splash and 'swim' in the bath. Both children have their own special qualities and unique gifts.

Is Kyle's seal gesture an expression of what stirred so deeply within his mother both before and almost immediately after his birth? Or is it something he carries within him from primordial times, even from Hyperborea, the 'land beyond the North Wind' as described in Greek mythology (known in geological terms as the Palaeozoic period)? A little conjecture may not be out of place here! Could it be that during her pregnancy, that most magical time in a woman's life, Dorothy awakened in the human spirit within her (Kyle), memories of a primeval life; and was it this which he unconsciously expressed in the seal gesture? These are mysteries which challenge our imagination, and reach far beyond our present theme. But we can say that Dorothy's pregnancy and Kyle's gesture allow us a brief glimpse of them.

## Dorothy and the Blue Birds

And now Dorothy herself writes ...

*Another experience I had was during a pregnancy prior to conceiving Kieran. This pregnancy only lasted twenty weeks and culminated in the spontaneous premature still-birth of twin boys. (We did not know we were expecting twins.) Halfway through this pregnancy I was resting in our garden. The day was beautiful: warm spring sunshine, fresh breezes, green leaves and blossoms. I became suffused by a quiet joy, and felt a little presence on top of both my shoulders. It was as though two blue birds had come to bring me a message. They stayed a little while, and then flew away. Remembering this experience helped me accept the pain of losing those two little boys. To accept and be able to surrender became for me a task which, once achieved, has stood me in good stead in many other situations.*

*In a way, those blue birds have never left me.*

# Jenny and the Birds

Jenny writes:

### Raina and the White Birds

*Mid-February 1980: We had been hoping and wishing to conceive our first child for a few months. One day I was out in our garden in Studley Park, Melbourne, and suddenly a white owl (I think it was a Tawny Frog-mouth) swooped down over me so close that one of its wings just touched my shoulder. It flew over to a nearby tree. I was deeply moved by the experience – it felt somehow very significant and I thought: 'I wonder if this means I'm pregnant?'*

*About a week later we were visited again over a few days – this time it was definitely a Tawny Frog-mouth. It would come and sit on the ledge of our verandah; it sat there for hours one night. Two weeks after this second run of visits I discovered that I was pregnant. The first visitation had therefore been a kind of annunciation, occurring just a few days after conception.*

*End of November 1980: A few weeks after our daughter Raina was born, I heard the sound of cockatoos in the garden. I looked outside and there were three white cockatoos flying around. They settled on our big tree – the same one the owl had first landed on. I had the same feeling of significance and I wondered what it meant – it somehow seemed to be some kind of welcome to Raina. She was exactly three weeks and three days old and I still wonder about the significance of the number three in her life.*

### Jesse and the eagles

*Three years later, we were settled into our new home in the country, on a farm in the mountains of northern New South Wales, Australia. We had begun to feel the calling to have another child. One day I was out in the garden, hanging out the washing and looking across at our magnificent mountain views when I heard some eagles calling overhead. I looked up and saw two eagles circling quite low – calling to each other, I thought. But as I watched them fly higher I saw that they were joined by five others so there were actually seven eagles flying the thermals above. (In twelve years of living here I have seen many eagles but never so many in a group.) Again I felt deeply moved, a sense of inner significance, and wondered whether this could mean I was pregnant again. Sure enough, a couple of weeks later I found out that I was pregnant with our son, Jesse.*

*I find these experiences almost unbelievable myself and yet they are indelibly printed on my memory. Now when I observe my children, aged 14 and 11, I can see something of the owl wisdom and the eagle wisdom reflecting in them. Also they both have a tremendous affinity with animals/wild creatures. Raina has a special capacity with horses – she can calm excited horses just talking to them. Jesse, even as a very young child, was always finding birds in the garden – they seemed to let him walk up to them and catch them, then he would just pat and cuddle them for a while and let them go. I am truly a fortunate mother.*

*Raina and Jesse feeding a baby fox*

# Michelle and the prophecies of Gus

Michelle writes:

*'Mummy, there's a baby in your tummy.'* We were both sitting on the
bed counting the birds in the tree outside the window.

Twelve silk angels spiralled above our heads. A few days later my
doctor confirmed that my son, Gus (who was not yet three), was right. I
was pregnant.

In the bleak winter weeks that followed, Gus and I both grew very ill,
and I could not help feeling that the baby had left us during this time. I
had sent invitations for Gus's birthday party at a Children's Farm,
determined that the celebration should go ahead. I sat near the fire in
the stone barn and wrapped my long coat around Gus. Visitors
congratulated me on the pregnancy, but I remained uncertain.

Exactly one month later I miscarried.

Three months passed, and then, 'Mummy, there's a baby in your
tummy.' So I said, 'Well, let's go and see the doctor.' Then we rugged up
against the frosty spring morning and walked to the surgery hand in
hand. I got a strong positive reading.

'When will our baby be born?' I asked Gus. 'On my birthday,' he
grinned. And he was right. Gus and Oscar were born on the same day,
four years apart – Geminis.

# 2

# Birthing

*Beloved Child, I welcome you*

Giving birth is a highlight in a woman's life, whether the birth be the first or the tenth. It is always a deeply moving experience of tumultuous body rhythms, of the presence of higher beings, and of holiness as a human being emerges to begin a new life on earth.

This unique experience makes it possible for a woman to reach a greatly heightened consciousness, a state of fulfilment not usually attainable in other ways.

Jane, Kristen and Cheryl have written of their experiences of giving birth. What they have said forms the content of this chapter.

## Jane experiences

*Writing of my birth experiences has taken a long time to sit down to do, because even the words in my head and my heart seem so inadequate after the births themselves. This is probably because birth is an experience of the spirit and soul not easily expressed in ordinary words. Here is my attempt. I cannot personally separate the births of my three children, each profoundly different, yet in retrospect, connected.*

*Very briefly, I think of Cal's (the first), as an experience of the 'God' within me.*

*Ruby's (the second), an experience of the 'God' outside me.*

*Jimmy's (the third), as the 'I' witnessing/communicating with inner and outer forces.*

Cal's birth was a very inner journey, one of enjoying the first part of first-stage labour almost in a meditation; then towards transition a very long, deep penetrating 'OM' type chant came from me (something I had not previously been able to do). During the whole of second stage I was silent. I was immensely aware of the power that every single cell of my body was exerting as I guided and massaged Cal's head down the birth canal with my finger. Without a doubt this was truly the greatest experience of my life. I felt so fulfilled, purposeful – and surely must have been the first woman to have ever given birth!

Ruby's birth was an 'out of body' experience from the beginning. In the first stage of labour, from 3 a.m. until 6.30 a.m.I had the visual and physical sense of lying on the water's edge at Wilsons Promontory (a rugged Victorian National park in southern Australia, surrounded by the waters of the Southern Ocean). As the contractions started, the waves seemed to come rolling in over me; as they rolled back into the ocean they pulled my cervix open a little more to allow the light of the full moon to shine into my body – and the moon really was full that night. Prior to this, I had had no success with visualisation.

I was extremely relaxed when I got up in the morning with Tony (my husband) and Cal, so advised the midwife that I was in no way in need of her and neither was there a likelihood of my giving birth soon (we had planned a home birth). I spent the next one and a half hours having breakfast and wandering around the garden with Cal and Tony. They watered the plants, and with each contraction I did gentle hip rotations up against trees and verandah posts. The midwife had told me to call her when something happened, or when I felt I needed her. When a contraction brought drops of fresh blood, I decided to call her. She said she was on her way, and if the baby arrived before she did, to wrap it warmly and nurse it.

I went into the bathroom with Tony, and with each contraction I opened my mouth and an operatic song came out, lasting the whole length of the contraction (with only one breath), and spiralling higher...and higher and higher. I was totally unaware of any physical sensation during this time, neither of labour pain or pushing in between contractions (there were not many). I was able to ask my girl friend to get some towels, and told my husband not to worry because I strongly sensed that angels were with us; and because I was standing, I asked *him to be sure to catch the baby, and to check that the cord was not around its neck. I turned around at one point to look at Tony. His face was streaming with tears, and he told me later this was because of the voice/song that I was singing. I remember feeling the baby's head, and telling Tony and Jan (my girl friend) that it was very close.*

*Ruby arrived very safely into Tony's hands, with her membranes intact. I had been concerned about contaminating the baby with thrush which I had throughout the pregnancy, off and on. Her arrival with membranes intact immediately allayed that anxiety. We wrapped her and I nursed her for a good ten or fifteen minutes before we peeked to see whether our new treasure was a little girl or a little boy; and it was 45 minutes of uninterrupted bliss on our own before the midwives arrived.*

*I could not sing a note before Ruby was born. I now sing to my children a lot, making up tunes for nursery rhymes and little songs, and this year singing Christmas carols. In fact, people now say that I can sing!*

*Ruby's birth was a truly humbling experience.*

*Ruby, an outdoor girl from the start*

*Jimmy was also born at home, and this time we made sure our extraordinarily wonderful midwife, Chris, and her assistant were there. I had also asked Tony and Chris to make sure I didn't end up huddled in our tiny bathroom, but was in our beautiful bedroom with the fire going. Cal and Tony had set it for us all in the morning. When I knew I was in labour, albeit very very gentle, I rang Chris at 3.00 in the afternoon, and continued hanging out washing and playing football with Cal in the garden. We showed Chris around our newly planted garden, and at 4.30 p.m. decided to go in and light the fire. I was very silent with the contractions, doing gentle hip rotations (belly dancing), feeling an immense peace, awe and wonder at what was going on in my body, while Cal, Ruby, Tony, the midwives and my friend Vasiliki watched. Between contractions I talked to my children, and as I moved into second stage I was able to tell them that the angels were pushing the baby out. Although I was much more physically aware with Jimmy's birth, I had an experience of knowing that angels are present at the birth of a baby – there was a part of me witnessing all that was going on. Jimmy was born at 5.30 p.m. and Tony caught him amid a gush of water. He too was born with his inner membranes intact. Cal and Ruby, just behind me, were able to see their little brother come into the world. Jimmy was the 830th baby whom Chris had delivered, and the first birth Vasiliki had attended.*

*I am so blessed to have been given these three children. Their births were the beginning of a most profound journey. They brought me to a recognition of a higher dimension of life, and my life is now so rich, so full of purpose, so supported. I learn (I hope) every day. In becoming a mother I learnt to value the present and to trust the future for myself and for our family.*

*Today, when it appears that the value of motherhood is at its lowest ebb, such knowledge and experience of motherhood is desperately needed. Its loss is not only a tragedy for children, but for the women who deny themselves this extraordinary gift.*

*I feel women need help in learning to value motherhood, and guidance and support in their mothering. I have found this so much easier through Steiner's knowledge of human development, particularly of the young child's wants and needs; and, very importantly, of how to communicate with her.*[1]

# Kristen welcomes Woody

*It is difficult to find words to convey the magical experience of the process of giving birth. I believe this is why I never completed the story I began to write not long after Woody's birth. I preferred to re-visit the experience within, rather than attempt to put pen to paper. But now, six months later, I can write the story.*

**Monday, 21st February**
*A cooler day; 22 C. – much welcomed after temperatures soaring into the high 30s. Feeling rather tired and sensing Woody's birth was near, I decided to change the sheets on the bed, light a candle and rest. Had a relaxing day, lounging around reading.*

*It was around 2.30 a.m.the following morning when I felt and heard a loud popping sound around my lower region. Could this be my waters breaking? Feeling a little apprehensive, I lay there motionless to await further signs. Then after a short time I felt a trickle of fluid run down my thigh. I slowly got out of bed and down it came. I called to Brian, my husband, and took a shower.*

*I was so excited – the journey had begun. We would soon meet the child who had been developing within me for the last nine months! It wasn't until I had dried and dressed myself that the contractions began. It was now 3.00 a.m. I didn't want to go back to bed as I knew this would slow down the process. The contractions were mild, so I made the bed and fiddled around in the kitchen. Brian began to pack the car ready for the trip to the Birthing Centre.*

*At this stage I re-read my goals for the labour – a gentle active labour using a number of different positions, kneeling, squatting etc. I wanted to use ujjayi *[2]* breathing, affirmations, and relaxation to manage the pain. I also called on the angels to be with us through the birth.*

*Around 4.30 a.m.we rang the midwife, Sue, to report I was in labour, that my contractions were ten minutes apart and increasing in intensity. She suggested that we stay put and call back when the contractions were five minutes apart.*

*Now I needed to kneel and lean over a pile of pillows on the lounge. As each contraction began, I closed my eyes, used the ujjayi breathing and to my amazement began to visualise myself sitting on my surfboard at my favourite beach, waiting to ride the wave. The conditions were perfect, and there was Brian ten times life-size with a crowd of people behind him, cheering as I took off. It felt exhilarating (only a surfer knows the feeling!). As each contraction began, so I would take off on a wave and ride it until the contraction subsided. The visualizations continued for about an hour. Was this the work of the water spirits? At 5.30 a.m. my contractions were five minutes apart – another call to Sue to arrange to meet at the Birthing Centre. We arrived at 6.00 a.m.and contractions became increasingly intense and longer.*

### Transition
*I continued with ujjayi breathing, and then I began to hear affirmations clearly within me – the voice of Rachael B, whose relaxation tapes on 'Birth' I had listened to numerous times prior to Woody's birth. Hearing her voice repeat the positive affirmations kept me focused and calm, releasing me from the sensation of each contraction. Sue at this stage began massaging my hips and thighs in an upward motion – a technique the Amish* [3] *use. This helped tremendously during the contraction, along with Rachael's voice.*

*Brian and Sue were timely with their encouraging words, just when Rachael's voice ceased to sound inside me! Brian positioned himself on the end of the bed and I knelt on the floor hugging his waist. I stayed there until Woody arrived. This was a great comfort, having the physical contact, giving me strength.*

### Second Stage
*This was quite scary as I felt I had absolutely no control. My body had the urge to push, and did so without my consent! Eye contact with Sue and more ujjayi breathing assisted me to focus.*

*In between pushing, the smiling faces of four special friends appeared who had given me such positive messages of their birthing experiences. It was as though they were guiding me, giving reassurance of how the birth was unfolding. I felt very peaceful.*

*During this stage Brian continued to remind me to send the energy down rather than releasing it through my mouth! I focused and followed the instructions. After half an hour of pushing, our doctor appeared in the room and whispered in my ear, 'I know it stings, but just one more push with all your might and you'll see your baby.' So I did.*

*Woody was born at 8.35 a.m. What a joyous moment!*

*Woody at 9 months*

# Cheryl and the Sistine Madonna

*When pregnant with our first child, I asked Joan what I could do spiritually to prepare myself for birth and to shield the unborn baby from intrusive outside influences. Joan gave a most unexpected piece of advice. She said that Rudolf Steiner had recommended that during pregnancy and birth women meditate on Raphael's painting, The Sistine Madonna. This is what she would advise.*

*Once my husband Michael had ordered a print and had it framed, I combined relaxation practice and contemplation of The Sistine Madonna for about 10 minutes a day from the end of the fifth month of pregnancy. The figures and motifs in the picture slowly became familiar. I made these comments in my diary just before labour began in earnest: 'The picture of Raphael's Madonna and Child has achieved a definite presence in our home during this gentle, special time. It hangs under the*

*The Sistine Madonna*

*skylight in the hallway – far too overpowering to suitably hang in any room. On Sunday night, when the early contractions began and I felt so excited that I thought I wouldn't sleep, the picture of the Madonna and her Child, her attendants and those angels, fused into the whole present mood of what was happening. This summoned a strength and calmness which would not have been of the same quality without Raphael's gift.'*

*As labour progressed we went to hospital and were settled into a delivery ward set up for LeBoyer births. Soft lighting enabled us to highlight the Madonna print – this marvellous picture commanded a mood which was novel but respected by everyone there.*

*I became fully absorbed inwardly with the pain of stronger contractions, and while relaxing and breathing deeply and slowly, was completely focused on The Sistine Madonna. Over the next 12 hours, in the heightened consciousness of birthing, the image of this holy, feminine being gave me a joyous revelation of her essence.*

*Michael had an inkling of my experience: 'Cheryl has been coping excellently – lying calmly on the bed and meeting each contraction with real force. She tells me that much of this force is derived from the Madonna, who occupies her own chair...'*

Having neither preconceptions about birthing (other than that it was mostly painful), nor knowing how the Madonna painting could assist, I was amazed at what unfolded. The spaces between contractions were sheer bliss, and as the pain ebbed, I soared into the realm of clouds where the Madonna stood. As the pain edged back, her gaze held steady, beyond compassion and understanding, unmoved by sorrow or joy. She stood on the verge of movement and looked towards me with absolute acceptance of all there is. Her being held my being. The picture became a shrine – the colours, light, forms, the shaded souls and the Madonna within the frame came alive with a warm, timeless, spaceless dimension, holding my total attention. Her enormous child was borne up effortlessly by her poised uprightness, even as she stood on a cloud. He was not relevant to my experience then, except to show her infallible strength and capacity.

For about half an hour, in transition, the waves of pain swamped my concentration, and I turned away from the Madonna in a chase for oblivion by rapid breathing. With pushing, ability to focus returned and the miracle of birth transformed into the astonishing reality of a newborn baby. Michael described the hours after the birth: *'Such a warm halo of spirit surrounded us and pervaded the room.'* The Sistine Madonna print had already lost its glow and her gaze was more distant, leaving me free but encompassed in wisdom. The glow was now around our newly born baby and the Madonna's blue and gold mantle of unconditional love was wrapped around Michael, the baby and me. Michael felt this too: *'I attempted the outside world later that evening but soon returned to the warmth of the fold – the contrast with the day's experience had turned the 'real' world cold.'*

When we were all home again, the print was hung in our bedroom where it became a visual meditational presence as we embarked on the labyrinth of parenthood. A couple of weeks after the birth I was able to reflect on what happened when I turned away from the Madonna and found nowhere to flee. For that time there was a sense of inwardly dying and it seemed *'at that point the birth became an initiation… an initiation into what I cannot yet define.'*

*Cheryl, Michael and their four children. Emrys, whose*
*birth Cheryl has described, is standing*

*It is 18 years since Emrys was born and the experience lives vividly in*
*my soul. Rose, Anna and Stefan have also been born, each birth adding*
*its unique experience of The Sistine Madonna. Each birth has also*
*brought its own images and lessons, showing me the challenges and*
*possibilities I can meet as the mother of each different child. These are*
*invaluable for understanding life's journey together. Always the 'mantle'*
*has been strongest during the first 6 weeks after birth, lifting at 3 years*
*and indiscernible after 7-8 years. Over the years we have had many*
*experiences connected with the picture – to do with our children, our*
*family and other people.*

*10 years ago, when I read Steiner's description of The Sistine*
*Madonna as a true image for the Christmas festival,*[4] *it inspired a talk I*
*gave at a Christmas gathering soon after. The next year, on Christmas*
*Day, Stefan was born at home – with the picture again present as a*
*guiding image. The birth was 3 weeks earlier than expected and*
*remarkably like Emrys' in length, time of day and intensity. Events had*
*conspired in an uncanny way to weave personal experience into the*
*universal birth festival of Christmas.*

With due preparation then, the advice to work with the image of *The Sistine Madonna* has revealed a spiritual path and awakening. This can be through conscious celebration of the Christmas festival once a year, and then also as it relates to every moment of our lives. This path can be a gift of grace, given, in this age of the individual, when women surrender themselves during birth and are guided to a conscious meeting with the spiritual world. Once initiated through birthing, and tested in the care of our young children, the journey seems to continue parallel with the changes in our relationship with them as they grow. The gateway was opened with them and we remain bound with them on this path which motherhood forges. Finding ourselves on unknown ground with our children, the guiding inspirations from their births shine like familiar stars in the night. And when I wonder what I am to make of this unknown territory where the forces of pregnancy, birth and early childhood have cast me ashore, leaving me to find my way once their waves and gusts have subsided, I turn to take my bearings and encounter the Madonna's unwavering gaze.

# 3
# Mothering

*Beloved Child, I encompass you*

Since very ancient times the mother figure has occupied a significant place in the religions and philosophies of mankind. In more recent times, poets and dramatists have been the ones who most clearly portrayed qualities pertaining to the mother. We will first look at some of these images and perspectives, then see how they form the basis for examining mothering qualities in modern life.

Let us start by going back several thousand years to India.[1] There we find two distinct types of people – the Aryans in the north and the Dravidians in the south. The former founded a patriarchal society, revering a Father God. Their holy books were the Vedas and Upanishads. The Dravidians founded a matriarchal society and revered a creating Mother Goddess. Their holy books, the Tantra, were devoted largely to the feminine aspects of religion and to the qualities of the Divine Mother. She was usually portrayed with child, and the mother and child on earth were seen as a manifestation of this exalted divine Being. A mother was therefore greatly revered, for through her creating and nurturing of the child she represented an earthly reflection of the creating Mother Goddess.

This attitude of respect and reverence was typical of the many matriarchal societies throughout the orient and in neolithic Europe. In China, the *Tao Te Ching* speaks of the 'mystic Mother', a figure greatly revered in ancient times.

The religions and the creation myths of ancient Europe were also mostly matriarchal. The story of Eurynome,[2] a Pelasgian creation myth is a typical example:

> Eurynome was the Goddess of All Things. In the beginning she arose out of Chaos, and because she could find no firm footing, she divided the sky from the sea. This filled her with delight, and she danced naked and wildly upon the waves. She used the North Wind to help her Creation Dance. She was seen by the serpent Ophion, who, becoming lustful, wound himself around her body, and she became pregnant. She assumed the form of a dove and laid the Universal Egg. Ophion curled himself around this, and Eurynome brooded it upon the rhythm of the waves. When the Egg hatched, it was found to contain all things in perfect harmony. Eurynome had transformed Chaos into an ordered harmony. She was delighted with the outcome of her work.

Many Greek myths, Orphic, Olympian, Homeric, depict a similar theme. For these ancient people, motherhood was the 'prime Mystery'.[3] It was always associated with a creative faculty which transformed chaos or night into harmony or day – just as a typical mother does today, coping with the demands of family life and attempting to create order out of an often chaotic family situation. The story of Eurynome illustrates this aspect of her work.

Many old cultures portrayed a Mother Goddess. We can think of Isis and her child Horus in Egyptian mythology; the Greeks' Demeter and her daughter Persephone; and Artemis of the Ephesians, the Mother Goddess whose ample bosoms fed the world – whose nature it was to give and succour.

We must now listen carefully to what the great Pythagoras[4] has to say, who lived about six centuries BC and was a man of immense wisdom. He had received education from the many centres of

learning of his day, not only in Greece, but as far afield as
Babylon, where the mighty teachers of the orient nourished the
souls of their students from deep founts of knowledge. Having
absorbed these rich experiences Pythagoras returned to Greece,
and later set up his famous school on the east coast of Italy.

He was sixty years of age when he married; but he had a
youthfulness of soul, a boundless energy – the fire of the spirit
shone from him. His wife, Theano, was much younger than he,
and was able to bear three children. The union of their lives and
the upbringing of their children gave Pythagoras penetrating
insights into family life and the place of the mother within it. His
profound teaching on the sacred nature of the mother's work
reveals the depths of his observation and understanding.

He described the mother as a priestess at the family altar. It
was her soul which perfumed the whole of family life. He regarded
her work as sacramental, for it was her task and responsibility to
prepare the future generation; and this could only be done
according to divine law. He saw her need for protection after the
birth of a child, and the infant's need too. He therefore established
the *gynaeceum* where both mother and child could be together,
undisturbed after the experience of birth. In writing of this,
Edouard Schuré explains:

> In order to cause the child to unfold properly, the kisses
> and caresses of the mother were considered necessary. The
> powerful enveloping love of woman is needed to defend
> the soul [from] the attacks of external life. Because in full
> consciousness she fulfilled these lofty functions,
> considered divine by antiquity, a woman (mother) was
> really the priestess of the family, the guardian of the
> sacred fire of life, the Vesta of the hearth.

Furthermore, Pythagoras established a special section for
women in his Institute. He recognised that through her
mothering, a woman had already achieved many of the
preparatory qualities needed for gaining a higher consciousness.
Again, Schuré explains:

By establishing a section for women in his Institute, Pythagoras refined and intensified what had existed before him. Through him, along with rites and precepts, the women initiates received the supreme principles of their function. Thus he gave to those who were worthy, the consciousness of their role. He revealed to them the trans-figuration of love... the interpenetration of two souls at the very centre of life and truth.

It is fascinating to explore the Pythagorean teaching on man and woman, but that goes beyond our theme (Chapter 12 looks at this subject in more depth). Let us content ourselves for now with one thought which this great man set before us: '... the perfect image of God is not man alone, but man and woman.'

The first three centuries AD saw the compilation of the Talmud. Hebrew scholars in Palestine and Babylon gathered together the laws pertaining to all aspects of their life. These included codes of conduct for women and the responsibilities of the mother. Rabbi Dr. Isidore Epstein has given a comprehensive overview of Judaism in his book of that title.[5] There we also find that the mother's task is regarded as being 'of a sufficiently sacred character to engage a woman's attention to the exclusion of any other religious duty...' and that the home was regarded as the most important institution for the individual. 'It is like a place of worship... and social service...' Here we have a similar view to that expressed by Pythagoras almost a thousand years earlier. The sacredness of the mother's task would seem to be a firmly established attitude of ancient teachers.

Indulging in something of an interlude, we will now transport ourselves to the court of the first Plantagenet king of England, Henry II, and his wife, Queen Eleanor, formerly of Aquitaine:

The Queen has just given birth to Prince Henry, the first of her four sons. But nowhere in the palace is there a wet-nurse to feed and care for the infant. Queen Eleanor has not engaged one, for she has insisted on breastfeeding and mothering the child herself! This is simply preposterous, unheard of, and all the ladies-in-waiting, and in fact, the entire court are appalled. Yet Queen Eleanor proceeds according to her plan. She breastfeeds and tends the child herself; and such is her joy and satisfaction that she does it again, and again and again, for her succeeding three sons.

Thus was established a strong basis for the valiant Plantagenet princes and their descendants! Among them was Richard Coeur de Lion, and Henry V of Agincourt fame. Is it unreasonable to muse upon their deeds of daring and ask oneself if Eleanor's influence (of spirit or genes?) was at work in them? It is an appealing thought.

In the Middle Ages, Dante wrote his allegorical masterpiece, *The Divine Comedy.* He portrayed himself as the universal sinner, one lost in the Dark Wood, seeking for the path to Paradise and the Blessed Virgin. There are a number of symbols in the poem, the one of direct interest to our theme being a quality epitomized in Beatrice. Dorothy Sayers, in a brilliant introduction to the Comedy,[6] speaks of Dante's description of Beatrice. For him she was 'the vehicle of glory', and he equated her qualities with those of the Blessed Virgin Mother. We meet her in Canto 2 of the Inferno, when Virgil relates to Dante her deed of sacrificial love. She had left her high exalted place in Paradise, and descended through Purgatory to Limbo in Hell to entreat Virgil's help for Dante. Beatrice, carrying the forces of the Divine Mother was 'swift to seek his good...' and 'from that high resting place to speed me down...' In this capacity for sacrifice, Beatrice expresses a quality of unconditional giving. Dante says of her that, for his sake, 'thou didst leave the imprint of thy steps in Hell'.

Finally, we come to Goethe – German poet, scientist and philosopher of the 18th and 19th centuries. Like Pythagoras, life had bestowed on him a wealth of experience, and he expressed this in his drama, *Faust*. As *The Divine Comedy* of Dante is a portrayal of the Sinful Soul, so in *Faust* Goethe depicts the Seeking Soul, pouring into it the wisdom of his years.

In Part 2 of the drama we meet with the Realm of the Mothers.[7] Faust obtains the key to this from Mephistopheles, and enters. He finds a realm of 'stupendous things (that) are deepest felt through awe'. Here one must transcend all things earthly to be able to behold the mysterious essence of the Mothers, they who work in formation and transformation. It is from this creative mother-essence that Faust will be able to awaken in his soul new powers. Penetration into this realm of creating power is described by Goethe as a 'journey to the Mothers'.

The final scene[8] of this great drama of the human seeking soul sums up Goethe's life-long fascination with the theme of Eternal Womanhood, the Divine Mother. He names her *Mater Gloriosa*, the Glorious Mother. It is she who with tender love receives the soul of Faust brought to her by angelic beings. It is she who soars aloft, encompassing all those who seek her love. Goethe describes her as having an eternal quality. This quality overcomes all 'earth's insufficiency', it 'wins life through love', and leads the human soul onwards and upwards. In the last verse of his great drama, a chorus of mystics speaks these words:

> All things corruptible
> Are but a parable;
> Earth's insufficiency
> Here finds fulfilment;
> Here the ineffable
> Wins life through love;
> Eternal Womanhood
> Leads us above

This is how Goethe – a man of most profound insights into life – observed and understood the characteristics of mothering.

Before going on, let us briefly re-state the viewpoint of those whose knowledge and breadth of vision should command our respect:

In the old matriarchal societies, the mother represented the creating Mother Goddess, and as such was worthy of reverence and respect. Greek creation myths portray the mother as one able to create and transform – the story of Eurynome is an example of this. For Pythagoras the mother was a priestess of the home, ministering to the souls of those in her care. He regarded this work as sacred, for it was she who carried the key to the future. Hebrew scholars of the 3rd and 4th centuries substantiated this view, and formulated it into the laws of the Talmud. We briefly visited Eleanor of Aquitaine and observed her devotion to her sons. She expressed her mothering by insisting upon breastfeeding them all herself. For Dante, Beatrice represented the quality of total giving, a sacrificial love of the highest order. He equated this with characteristics of the Divine Mother. For Goethe, mothers have a creating and transforming power such as is met with in the Greek creation myths; and the Glorious Mother of the last scene of Faust represents all that is of an eternal nature, all that fulfils through love.

# Mothering Today

Using all this as a background, let us now turn to mothering *nowadays*. Do we find in today's mother any of the qualities recognized and revered in former times?

Let us look first at the Beatrice quality of **giving,** a capacity for sacrifice expressed in deeds: mother-love shows itself in many forms, expressing itself in deeds, words, tenderness and so on. (We explore it further in a later chapter.) Motherly deeds of love are expressed in the daily round of tasks, and in frequent sleepless nights, tiredness, no time for oneself. This is a sacrifice, which, as we will see later, is an exalted form of love, a total giving, asking nothing in return. In breastfeeding, the mother unconditionally gives the forces of her own life contained in abundance in her milk. This is a unique form of sacrificial love, specific to mothers. We will have much to say about it a little later. At the level of mother-love, **feeling becomes cognitive.** Mother comes to **know** through the heart, rather than through the intellectual rationalism of the head. The cognitive capacities of mother-love are frequently looked upon derisively by a society which places prime value on intellectual achievement. It is worth noting that Solomon, the very epitome of wisdom, says, 'I applied mine heart to know wisdom.' [9]

But mothering is more than giving. It is also the joy of **receiving.** Joy, like love, expresses itself in a diversity of forms, shows many faces. There is the joy of communication – smiling at each other; and there is the joy of going for walks together, making discoveries, noticing the fresh budding of plants, rejoicing in colours, singing nursery rhymes together, listening, and sharing special secrets. These are some of the many joys of receiving. They are experiences to be treasured, for they are like a fountain of refreshing water for a mother's soul.

And we must add another quality – of **encompassing.** We find it in Goethe's Mater Gloriosa, Dante's Virgin Mother, the Pythagorean description of mother who encompasses the family as she presides at the family altar. It is a horizontal, enfolding gesture. Willie Sucher in his book *Cosmic Christianity*[10] speaks of the 'Washing of the Feet' as taking place on the horizontal plane. He describes this plane as portraying 'the principle of the Brother', one which overcomes the vertical social structure and establishes the horizontal order of brotherhood. In her daily activities of encompassing children and wider family, mother makes this horizontal gesture. As she gives and receives with love, she adds this to the human vertical. It is an awe-inspiring gesture. We will see later that a future humanity, striving to establish a new order of life, will look to the community (the brother/sister), not to the isolated individual for its way forward. Mother's encompassing skills are a beacon which points to the future.

*Jill (mother) encompassing at Penny's second birthday party*

Yet there is still more – the **creative aspect** of mothering, the Eurynome quality in the context of the Greek myth. While both mother and father create the home, it is usually mother who, like the ancient Creator Goddess, arises out of chaos and is able to bring a breath of new harmony to the home situation. For example, it is usually she who creates the home festivals, the seasonal rituals, encourages children to make an autumn table, helps to gather feathers, twigs, leaves, shells and a host of other treasures. These are some of her creating, transforming deeds which recall the Goethean 'Realm of the Mothers'.

Finally, there is the bond of a **shared destiny.** Between a mother and her children the thread of destiny connects strongly. In olden times this was called 'the law of karma', and was seen as a means of resolving much from the past, as well as establishing something new for the future. This, of course, applies to father too, but the intrinsic quality of a mother's love is of a different nature to a father's. The act of accommodating the child within

*Margaret and Christopher add to the summer table,*
*while Nicholas is absorbed in his book*

one's own body, of going through the birth process, of giving one's
own life force in the breast milk, all of this activates the mother's
feeling life to a degree well beyond the usual human experience.
Such strengthened heart forces, working into the knotted
entanglements of destiny, can transform the old and create the
new. The mother-child relationship connects with soul-spiritual
laws that govern our universe and work into our daily life.

Considering all these things, one can truly say that mothering
nowadays *does* still embrace many of the mother qualities
recognized and revered by an ancient wisdom; and that its
transforming power can enable a warming glow to enlighten what
is often experienced as the barren wilderness of modern life.

# 4
# Dear Joan...

*Beloved Child, I write of you*

## Letter from Melinda

The following letter was written by Melinda after a lecture on mothering given by the author at 'The Vital Years' seminar[1] held in Melbourne, Australia in 1995. Melinda Turner is the mother of two boys, aged 3¹/4 years and 9 months. She has attended the Gabriel Baby Centre[2] with them both. She is a school teacher by profession, and has completed a teacher training course in Steiner education. Both boys are booked in to attend the Melbourne Rudolf Steiner School. Melinda has founded a Mothers' Support Group which gives opportunity for like-minded mothers to meet together on a regular basis. Mothering is currently her full-time vocation.

*Dear Joan*

*I wanted to write to say once again how very much I appreciated your talk on mothering. It gave me so much encouragement and inspiration. As you said, there is very little respect or support for mothering in our society, and I confess this really does get me down at times. Although I know the worth of what I'm doing and have the support of my husband, Bruce, it is hard that mothering is held in such low regard by the rest of society, even including some people whom I know well. I think the worst comment I've had to deal with yet was being told by someone that what I'm doing is 'such a waste of your qualifications'.*

*Melinda, Bruce, Sam and William after a day's work in the garden*

*As you pointed out on Saturday night, mothering is such a wonderful path of self-growth and spiritual maturing. Like you, I too know of no other activity a woman can undertake to develop her feminine qualities of sacrificial love, gracious receiving and enfolding. For me, mothering is **the** most challenging and deeply rewarding work I've yet done. As it can so often seem a lonely and sometimes thankless path, it is wonderful to receive encouragement. You have been a major source of support and encouragement to me in conversations we've had during my visits with the boys to the Gabriel Centre. I feel that your wonderful talk – with its great wealth of historical and literary information – will be an ongoing source of nourishment to me in my mothering. When I am feeling overwhelmed by the chaos of home life, I will remember Eurynome transforming the chaos into order and harmony, and, like her, I will be proud of and pleased with my efforts. The Pythagorean image of the mother as the priestess at the family altar has also struck me very deeply. And I shall no longer feel occasional pangs of resentment that I am the one who* always has to organize the birthday celebrations, festivals and picnics. What a difference it makes to realize that that is my sacred task and that no one can fulfil this role as I can. I don't know if I'm expressing myself well but these small shifts in perspective make all the difference.

So thankyou dear Joan. Hearing you speak about the value of what I and other mothers do, has been an incalculable blessing. I walked out of your talk feeling powerful and wonderful! What you said is real treasure to me, and to all the other Gabriel mothers, and to our children – and through us (bearing in mind Eleanor of Aquitaine!) to the rest of the world.

With love and gratitude
Melinda

*Melinda*

## Thoughts from Jane

Jane Watson is the mother of three children, aged $5^1/_2$, $3^1/_2$ and 8 months when this was written. She has attended the Gabriel Baby Centre with all the children, and has made a study of Rudolf Steiner's teaching including his outline of the human being. She and her husband Tony live in an outer Melbourne suburb, and the children are booked in to attend the Melbourne Rudolf Steiner School. To gain insight into this type of schooling, she has attended a part-time teacher training course in Steiner education.

Dear Joan
Here are some thoughts that came to me after our last conversation. I would like to share them with you.

It seems to me that mothering is much more than 'bringing up' the children. I have experienced it in a much deeper sense – I would say, a holy sense. As you know, I feel quite passionate about these deeper aspects, and regard it as tragic that many mothers today are totally misled about these things. What a tragic loss for them! I wrote down these thoughts after thinking about my own situation, and what I am learning from my mothering years. I count myself greatly blessed to be having this experience. I thought you would like to hear what I have come to!

Much love and appreciation,
Always – Jane

*Being a mother can be an experience of the 'Washing of the Feet'. It involves sacrificial, unconditional love, giving over of the self to the needs and care of the child. When done willingly with no desire for any returns, there can be an experience of immeasurable joy and bliss. This comes from just being with the little ones who are still so closely connected to heaven. The more one gives of oneself, the more one receives. This is a miracle. There is no limit to receiving, just as there is no limit to giving.*

*My mothering has been made immensely rich by having an under-standing of the children which extends beyond their physical being – that is, a Steiner orientated perspective of a child's life and development. From my experience of breastfeeding I have come to a deeper appreciation of this. I feel that when I am feeding my baby we make a cross – that is, I sit upright, and my baby lies across me in the horizontal.*

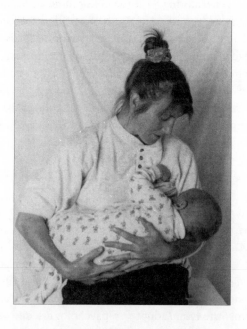

*Jane and Jimmy breastfeeding make a cross*

*Is this part of the 'I AM' and Washing of the Feet experience? I feel sure
it is! To choose not to breastfeed, and not to appreciate the value of
motherhood, as is common in the modern world, is to forfeit this gift.*

*I have been thinking about our studies and what Rudolf Steiner has
said about preparing the future;[3] how we must work to overcome
divisiveness amongst brothers, families and nations. To deny or
undervalue motherhood seems to be creating a divisive/dark space in
the fundamental fabric of human relationships – that is, mother and
child, the first or beginning of all relationships.*

*As you know, our children are now living in their first stage of
development outside the womb – that is, their first seven years. I have
come to realize that it is no accident that this time lays the foundation
for the future development of will. From my studies and observations of
the children, I now understand how important it is to know this and to
be able to guide them in a right way. I remember we talked about how
the will, when penetrated by thinking, creates purpose, initiative,
motivation and direction; and how, without a well-developed will, we
cannot use our feelings or the intellect, no matter how developed they
are. I feel it is like laying good foundations for a house and having an
understanding of its purpose. I try to apply this analogy to my children's
development, especially to the burgeoning of their strong will! I have
found that to have some understanding of these things makes it possible
to practise appropriate mothering in these early years. Of course, the
children's behaviour changes once they start at kindergarten and later at
school. What then is the legacy of these first seven years?*

*These are my musings on our recent conversation.*

## Reflections from Jan

Jan Bricknell, as her letter sets out, worked for a number of years
in the corporate world. Her mother had died when she was ten
years of age, and she grew up in a male household of father and
three brothers, feeling a lack of any real feminine nurturing. To
cope with this, she later 'adopted a psychological suit of armour'.
It was during the birth of her son, Nicholas, that she felt she was
able to shed this armour and become a woman, and this enabled
her to make the further transition to 'mother'.

*Dear Joan*

*At our last visit to the Gabriel Centre, you told me you were engaged in writing a book on mothering; and we spoke briefly about being a mother and compared it to a woman's experience in the corporate world. I would like to elaborate on this subject in this letter. Having seen both sides of the coin so to speak, I feel I may have something to contribute on the matter.*

*I guess I would consider myself as being typical of younger women today. Like others, I received the message that the purpose of a successful life was to establish a career and just enjoy all of the trappings it could provide. When asked whether I would have children, my reply would always be vague – there was some intention of having children 'down the track', but I was not sure at all where they fitted into the scheme of things.*

*So, having obtained my university degree, I secured a position as a consultant in one of the world's leading professional partnerships. This was it – I was on my way.*

*To be successful in corporate life it is necessary to use masculine qualities because the world of business was forged by and is ruled by men. Sure, there was equal opportunity, but it did not mean changing the ground rules, nor changing the way business was done. Life revolved around the rational and the intellectual, and decisions were made according to the cold, hard facts.*

*I worked hard and was, I now realise, very ambitious. Both within and outside the firm, life was competitive, so in the end you considered yourself lucky if you didn't have to work all day on Saturday and some of Sunday. Life was fairly unrelenting and hard nosed and geared towards achievement.*

*If you couldn't stand the heat, no one was going to hold your hand, you just had to get out of the kitchen (or more commonly, work longer hours). Here, emotions held no place whatsoever. There was absolutely no time to smell the roses.*

*How did I feel? Well, much of the time I didn't. I just felt pretty numb. I lived my life in an unconscious manner. It just didn't seem real. But I do remember feeling, when I managed to take the time to reflect, an enormous sense of emptiness and of desperate loneliness, like something really important was missing from my life. I would often* attempt to fill this gap with diversions – restaurants, shopping, clubs – but these distractions, in the end, provided no relief.

The world at this time in my life seemed like a big, scary and antagonistic place, with pressures and conflict everywhere. Nothing appeared safe or secure. I guess I felt under siege. Being an 'independent woman' meant that emotionally there was no one to turn to. My armour had gone up and no one had managed to break through. It all felt very unforgiving. There was plenty of food for the ego, but no nourishment for the soul.

Five years later I found myself holding in my arms my first child and the joys and rewards of this experience are beyond words. When my son smiles, rays of sunshine fill my heart. My being is brimful of unconditional love for him, of connectedness and often of pure bliss. The rewards of growing a balanced and happy child are there to see. Which is not to say it is all wonderful. The physical, mental and emotional challenges are hard, often pushing me to the limit. Chaos often reigns and I'm constantly having to cope with change.

My journey towards motherhood was above all a journey inward. It began long before the recent birth of my first child and indeed long before I even conceived. It was a journey towards unlocking my inner world and rediscovering my feminine. I reclaimed my womanhood from a corporate world where I had denied it in order to fit in. It seems that to complete this transition to motherhood it was necessary for me to let go of my career, my ambitions and all the trappings of the lifestyle I was leading. It meant letting go of all the expectations from within and without. This has undoubtedly been a positive step.

Becoming a mother for me has been a wonderful catalyst for inner growth – above all, questioning my ability to love and nurture myself, so I will be capable of loving and nurturing another, to whom I am primarily responsible. Having a child has also meant readdressing my own childhood – its unresolved issues and patterns. It is a painful process, but brings with it deeper understanding.

It has also meant meeting the challenges and opportunities inherent in isolation and solitude, and the introspection this brings. There is little of the 'busy-ness' and distractions of my previous lifestyle which allowed me to ignore searching for a deeper meaning. This is partly because of the physical isolation many mothers, including myself, *experience. We no longer have strong community bonds and I often go the whole day without seeing or speaking to another adult. Where previously life revolved around socialising, meeting new people, conversations and other diversions, now there is only me and a little child of four months of age.*

*Becoming a mother has also meant re-examining my attitudes to myself as a woman and as a mother, because the overriding message I get from 'out there' is, that to be worthwhile, one must go out into the world and achieve, work, have a successful career. Mothering is not a valid occupation; pride is often the furthest thing from your mind when asked at a gathering 'So, what do you do?' Inherently, deep down, I don't believe any of this, but it's hard not to let it affect you when it has been ingrained almost every day of your life in a thousand subtle ways. I believe mothering is not held in high regard because it totally embodies a feminine energy which is all about nurturing and being. Becoming a mother has meant accepting that 'being' is as valid a state as 'doing', if not more so, due to its rarity. Despite this, I still often find myself judging my daily life by how much I achieve, not just accepting that much of the value comes from simply **being there** for my child.*

*Despite the messages I receive from outside, inside there is an inner knowing that what I am doing now is worthwhile, because I am 'front line', creating the next generation to caretake this planet. There is no substitute for taking the time to care and nurture. I sense that squeezing motherhood in between a career and other demands in no way equates to committed, thoughtful, full- time mothering. It is a quality thing, and that takes time to achieve. Consequently, I could not consider returning to work. Providing my child with a sense of belonging, a foundation of safety and security, and the warmth a loving home brings, is just too important. I believe these almost intangible qualities are also vitally necessary to help children grow inwardly and meet the challenges of the world today.*

*I have found moving into motherhood enormously challenging. There is the birth itself, the isolation, the lack of value society places on the mother's role, the uncertainty, the changes and the sacrifice. I do not blame women for literally throwing the baby out with the bath water and returning to work; on the surface motherhood is not a very attractive proposition! But I do believe that by denying motherhood we, as* women, are also throwing away one of the greatest opportunities to reconnect with the essence of what and who we really are. I believe that in joining the rush to become the highest achievers in the business world, we are literally 'cutting off our nose to spite our face'. We are ignoring the value both of ourselves as women and of one of the most important jobs there is. In chasing the 'Corporate Nirvana' myth (the greatest perpetrated in the twentieth century perhaps?) we women are also turning our backs on the opportunity to restrengthen the feminine element – the nurturing element which is desperately needed to restore the entire planet to its own equilibrium.

Like all situations in life, one can either use the experience productively to grow and develop or turn away from the challenge and wither. I have found that, like all great leaps of the soul, choosing motherhood entailed going against the norm and **consciously** questioning the road I was going down. I am glad I have taken this road.

With love and light
Jan Bricknell

October 1995

# 5

# Breast Feeding

*Beloved Child, I connect you*

'Breastfeeding is superior to any other form of feeding for the human infant.' So says Dr Desmond Gurry, Senior lecturer in Paediatrics at the University of Western Australia.[1] His statement reflects what mothers have always known in their hearts. Yet about forty years ago, in the 1950s and 60s, the number of infants fully breastfed during their first six months of life was perilously low. For mother had been persuaded that it didn't really matter whether baby was breastfed or not. As long as the substance of the food was much the same as breast milk, it would nourish the child just as well. So began the age of 'infant formulae' and all its attendant experimentation,[2] embodying a totally materialistic attitude which considered only the physical substance of the milk. Many mothers succumbed to this new advice, while others questioned its accuracy.[3] Fortunately for the human species, breastfeeding has now regained its rightful place. It has come to be recognized as 'superior to any other form of feeding for the human infant', and can therefore be regarded as a most important part of mothering.

There are many facets of this womanly art. There is the chemical substance of the milk (physical aspect), the comfort and happiness it gives to mother and baby (soul aspect), and also what can be described as the spiritual aspects of breastfeeding, which connect to areas of life inaccessible to ordinary scientific investigation. In this chapter our exploration will lead us from earthly substance to realities of spirit. Let us start with the material reality of substance.

# Substance

The milk of mammals shows wide variation in its chemical composition. The milk of those creatures which grow rapidly has a high protein and mineral content, so that the young body not only increases in size, but also hardens as it grows. Human milk, on the other hand, has a *low* protein and mineral content, enabling the child to increase in size very gradually, and the body tissues to remain comparatively soft. We can see this in the softness of the infant's bones and first teeth.

For example, baby rats with 12% protein and 2% minerals in the mother's milk, double their birth weight in six days after birth; sheep with 5.5% protein and 1% minerals, in ten days; the human infant, on the other hand, with 1% protein and 0.2% minerals in the mother's milk, takes 150 days to achieve this.[4] The table below sets out the percentage of protein and mineral content contained in a few selected mammalian milks.[5]

| | **Percentage:** | | |
|---|---|---|---|
| **Mammal** | **Protein** | **Mineral** | **Reference** |
| Human | 1.0 | 0.2 | Macy 1953 |
| Orang-utan | 1.1 | 0.2 | Schumacher 1934 |
| Chimpanzee | 1.2 | 0.2 | Ben Shaul 1962 |
| Squirrel monkey | 3.0 | 0.2 | Ben Shaul 1962 |
| Cow | 3.5 | 0.7 | From Hambraeus |
| Goat | 3.3 | 0.6 | "          " |
| Sheep | 5.5 | 1.0 | "          " |
| Donkey | 2.0 | 0.5 | 'Lactation' [6] |
| Domestic rabbit | 13.9 | 1.8 | Davis et al & others 1964 |
| Eastern cottontail | 12.5 | 2.0 | ? |

It will be seen from the above that only the higher apes, orang-utan and chimpanzee (unfortunately, no figures are available for the gorilla), have milk whose protein and mineral content is in any way comparable to that of human beings. This is not surprising – the infant chimpanzee, for example, looks almost human. As Hermann Poppelbaum points out, it has 'a skull whose form is at first clearly reminiscent of human proportions... The newborn ape still has a beautifully domed skull...'[7] Once the infant ape is weaned from its mother's milk, usually at about 12 to 18 months, it inexorably begins to take on the characteristics and appearance of the mother beast.

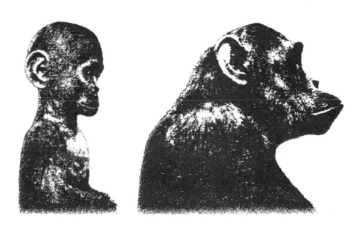

*from 'Man and Animal', H. Poppelbaum (see note 7)*

The only domestic animal whose milk is comparable to that of the human is the donkey (see table above). Yet it still has double the amount of protein and mineral contained in human milk.

As the table shows then, milk from other mammals contains a considerably greater quantity of substances which promote rapid growth and hardening, thus preparing the young animal for its life under the sway of earthly forces. The flexibility and plasticity of the human body, on the other hand, has enabled the human being to develop a consciousness which embraces both the earth and the spirit.[8] Mother's milk, with its low protein and mineral content is one factor which has contributed to the human body remaining flexible over many millennia.

## Soul aspects of breastfeeding

At the soul level, breastfeeding can best be described as a love affair between mother and baby. There is an intimacy here, a joyous interpenetration of soul with soul expressed outwardly in stroking, patting, cuddling, giving and receiving. Breastfeeding gives untold comfort and reassurance to the baby's soul, while for the mother it consists of an outpouring of protective love. It nourishes the soul of both, uniting mother and baby in a bond of enduring love.

But we must look further to come to the real core and meaning of breastfeeding. We must go beyond body and soul, and penetrate right into the heart of the matter. There we will find profound esoteric secrets about the real essence of mothering. Let us now address these mysteries.

## Spiritual aspects of breastfeeding

We will begin by considering the location of the human lactation glands (the breasts) on the body. They are over the heart region. If we divide the body into two poles, upper and lower, we see that the former is connected with our 'higher life', while the latter connects us firmly to the earth. To be human, we need both.

In the upper pole of the body we find: the heart – the physical seat of feeling; our thinking organ, the brain; lungs – the organs of breath; and the larynx which uses the breath to form articulate speech. The hands are also in the upper pole of the body. We use them in prayer, to bless, to caress, and for our creative activities. When we compare the creative potential of the hand with the limitations of the foot, we are immediately struck by the enormous difference. Our hands, heart, lungs, and our whole head organization connect and open us to a higher, spiritual realm of life. In the activity of breastfeeding, mother and child are connected with spiritual forces.

The lower pole of the human body connects strongly with earth forces: our digestive system into which we pour earth substance; the system of excretion using kidneys, lower intestines and bowel; reproductive organs connected with the life of earthly passions; and our feet with which we walk upon the earth. Through the lower pole of the body we are earth beings.

In the majority of mammals, the lactation glands are placed in the hind quarters – equivalent to the human body's lower pole. The horse, goat, sheep, cow, giraffe etc. are examples of this. Only the higher apes are an exception, which is understandable when we consider the picture, above, of the infant chimpanzee. Here there is a glimpse of the human, as though the radiance of the sun shone full of promise for one brief moment, only to be clouded in darkness as the beast gains the upper hand. In all other cases the young animal is destined from the beginning to be anchored to the earth. The placement of the lactation glands on the animal's body gives a compelling picture of this.

Returning to the upper pole of the human body, let us consider the heart, with which many mysteries are associated. It is the physical organ of human love (feeling), just as the brain is the physical organ of thinking. The heart's rhythm also connects us to the whole cosmos, to the solar rhythm. In his book, *Anthroposophical Medicine,* Victor Bott explains this in some detail.[9] He says:

> Human rhythms are related to cosmic rhythms...[the human respiratory rhythm] of 18 breaths per minute, gives 25,920 per day...which is the duration of the Platonic year expressed in terrestrial years. [If we divide this by 12]... we come to the Platonic month of 2160 terrestrial years which is the mean time which the vernal point takes to travel through one constellation of the Zodiac.

A further division by 30 into a cosmic day gives the figure 72. This, in terrestrial years, is the average human life span. It is also the average number of human heart beats per minute:

> In this way we may understand how the (human) cardiac rhythm is connected with the solar rhythm.'[10]

In breastfeeding, mother and child are in rhythmic tune with the whole cosmos.

We come then to the blood, pulsating through the heart, oxygenated through the lungs, bringing the warmth of life to the whole body. As Goethe indicated in Faust, blood is a most mysterious fluid; and Dr Pfeiffer describes it as 'containing the entire biological and physiological biography of the body'.[11] It is little wonder that Mephistopheles insists that Faust sign the contract with his own blood.[12] In October 1911 Rudolf Steiner gave a deep and far-reaching lecture on *The Etherisation of the Blood,* speaking of the esoteric processes associated with its transformation into etheric substance.[13] An elaboration of this theme is well beyond the scope of this book, but it is enough for us to see that the place of the human breasts over the heart region elevates breastfeeding well beyond soul and physical levels. The heart and its pulsating blood are related to lofty spiritual and cosmic processes, and it is these which surround the breastfeeding couple.

Jane, who has three children, is well aware of these mysteries. As she breastfeeds her baby, she is aware of making a cross. The baby forms the horizontal plane, and Jane, sitting in her chair, forms the vertical. She found this reality herself. It was a deeply moving discovery for her.[14]

It is also significant that the baby's sucking rhythm is in tune with the mother's heart beat. The following figures show this. Melinda found that her pulse rate when sitting was in the high 60s or low 70s; and when busy, high 70s or low 80s. Her baby's sucking rhythm, tested over a three day period, averaged 75 to 77 sucks per minute.

| Time per minute | No of baby's sucks | Mother's pulse rate |
|---|---|---|
| am | 64 to 80 | mid 70's |
| pm | 80 | mid 70's |
| pm | 73 to 79 | mid 70's |

Karen's figures reveal the following: mother's average pulse rate over two days, was 72 per minute. This was taken immediately after the baby had suckled. Average number of baby's sucks per minute over five feeds, extending over two days, was 68 per minute.

| Time per minute | No of baby's sucks | Mother's pulse rate |
|---|---|---|
| am | 49 to 60 | – |
| pm | 59 to 83 | 76 |
| pm | 41 to 80 | 66 |
| am | 41 to 66 | 70 |
| am | 53 to 76 | 76 |

Jane's figures yield much the same result:

| Time | No of baby's sucks | Mother's pulse rate |
|---|---|---|
| Over 24 hours | 72 to 80 | 70 |

But there is more. There are the **numbers** associated with the entire breastfeeding process: the three main numbers associated with lactation are 5, 12, and 40. What is to be learnt from this?

There are **five** stages of breastfeeding –
  the colostrum stage
  the coming in of the milk
  the establishment period (up to approximately 3 months)
  the established lactation period
  weaning from the breast.

Here is the substantial, bodily part of breastfeeding, for 5 is the number of the human body (head, two arms, two legs, symbolized by the five-pointed star.)

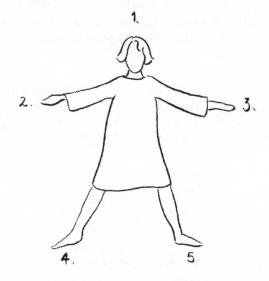

The number 12 relates to cosmic and spiritual aspects of life. For example, there are 12 signs of the Zodiac, 12 tribes of Israel in ancient Hebrew times, the 12 petalled 'lotus flower' (chakra) in the heart region, and Christ's choice of 12 disciples. How is this figure related to breastfeeding?

The traditional time for weaning from the breast was nine months – approximately 40 weeks. Today, many mothers feel that they are not ready to wean at this time. Using the 'cognitive feeling' mentioned in chapter 3, they find that they want to continue for two or three months more. This means that the weaning process *begins* when the baby is nine months of age; mother then gradually reduces the number of breast feeds, and at approximately twelve months the baby becomes fully weaned. This choice of 12 months for weaning is a *conscious* decision for many mothers today. It differs from the previous traditional practice of 40 weeks, in that it is a number which perceptive young women have consciously found for themselves. In so doing, they arrive at what is relevant for the present time, and connect themselves and their child to a number related to the spirit – the number 12. It is a telling choice! It is worth noting that for the foundation stone of the first Goetheanum building in Dornach, Switzerland,[15] Rudolf Steiner chose the form of a double pentagonal dodecahedron – expression of both the 5 and the 12, that is, the earthly human being and the spirit.

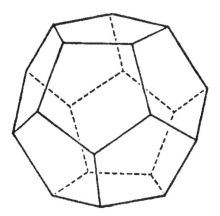

*Double pentagonal dodecahedron*

Let us now look again at the number 40. Forty weeks, as we have seen, was the traditional time for weaning from the breast. Today it remains relevant as a *starting point* for this process. Forty is a figure which leads into new and often challenging states of consciousness, opening up possibilities for the individual soul, the nation or the race. We see it manifesting in the individual today as the so called 'mid-life crisis'. This is often like a fiery conflagration in the soul, but it gives opportunity for new growth as the old gives way to the new. It could be more accurately called 'the mid-life opportunity'! Many other examples could be given, especially those recorded in the Old and New Testaments: the journey of the Children of Israel from slavery in Egypt to the promised land of Palestine, taking 40 years; and in the New Testament, the period of 40 days between the Resurrection and the Ascension, and of the Temptation. The metamorphosis of the weaning period, from 40 weeks to 12 months, can be seen as a reflection of these profound transformations of consciousness. Humanity strives forward to establish the new; and mothering, as practised today by many conscious young women, can contribute to this process.

In this chapter we have outlined aspects of breastfeeding not usually considered in assessing its value. We have gone beyond physical and soul aspects to consider the placement of the human breasts on the upper part of the body, over the heart region. This has led us to look at the heart rhythm and its connection with cosmic rhythms, the baby's sucking rhythm, the horizontal and the vertical as manifest in the activity of breastfeeding, and the significance of the numbers 5, 12 and 40 as they apply to lactation and to weaning from the breast. Much more could be said about these higher aspects of breastfeeding; but enough has been given to indicate its special importance.

When we consider all these things, we gain insight into the truth of Pythagorean wisdom about the mother. We understand how she is, indeed, a priestess at the home altar, undertaking a sacred task, needing the special recognition which Pythagoras bestowed on her. This can enable our understanding of mothering to expand into a vision of its true worth and meaning.

# 6

# Milks for Weaning

*Beloved Child, I enliven you*

After the child is weaned from the breast, the question of milk from another source arises. As we saw in the previous chapter, many mothers nowadays wish to breastfeed until the child is about one year old. Therefore it is usually in the child's second year that another form of milk becomes essential. By that age the little one is having a variety of foods that give a real connection to the earth, especially vegetables. This is an incarnating process, and it needs to proceed in an appropriate way. The careful introduction of food is one way of achieving this, for it goes without saying that the physical body needs to be adequately nourished if it is to grow and remain in good health. Mother is therefore faced with two important matters related to the choice of milk – one, she needs a milk which makes it possible for the child to grow into life on earth in an unhurried way, and also one that enlivens and nourishes the body to an optimum degree. It is this latter which we will now consider.

Let us look first at formula feeding. The use of these milks has grown enormously since people started to seek answers to everything within the domain of material substance, denying the reality of other realms – including that of life itself. From the point of view of infant feeding, this has been a catastrophe.[1] As was pointed out in the book *The Incarnating Child* (chapter 10), nutrition consists not of substance only, but of *enlivened* substance;[2] and the forces of life which work into substance (matter) are not the product of mineral particles – they do not originate there, but issue from a realm of universal life.[3] One can say that there is a realm of matter *and* a realm of life which in the organic kingdoms work together to produce living substance. Any observant and questioning person who has made a compost heap will gain some insight into life forces.

Milk is a living food consisting of matter and life force only, not soul. It therefore has a plant-like quality, free from the realm of feelings and animal nature. It is of prime importance that mothers understand these facts, so that they can choose a milk which will be appropriate for their children.

This brings us to consider the different milks available today. The main ones used are cows' milk formula, soya milk, goats' milk, rice milk, almond milk and fresh cows' milk. It is a formidable array from which mother must choose! She may ask whether the 'processing' of a product, whether it be milk or any other food, has an adverse effect on that product's *life force?* It is a crucial question which today's natural science cannot answer, for it is only able to analyse chemical composition. A spiritual science is needed to answer such questions.

# Cows' milk

If mother decides to use a milk which has not undergone 'processing', then there is biodynamic or organic unhomogenised fresh cows' milk or fresh goats' milk. Cows' milk has become suspect today as being mucus forming or causing other allergic conditions. However, we would do well to take to heart what Dr. Desmond Gurry[4] has to say about this. In an article published in 'Patient Management', in May 1989, he says:

> A genuine allergy, for instance to cows' milk, (or soy milk), should always be proven. Extensive elimination diets entered into on trendy and feeble grounds are to be deplored. This especially applies to atopic children with asthma and eczema.

Nevertheless, if fresh cows' milk is the one of mother's choice, it is prudent to introduce it to the child *gradually*. This can be done in the following way:

When the baby is seven months of age, add one drop of biodynamic unhomogenised cows' milk to the morning oatmeal porridge or other cereal, increasing by one drop each second day until reaching one household teaspoon of milk (5ml). There are roughly 40 drops to a teaspoon depending on the size of the dropper. This means that the child will be having a teaspoon of cows' milk by about 10 months of age. If there are no indications to the contrary (mucus, skin rash or asthmatic symptoms), then increase the quantity of milk by $1/2$ teaspoon (2.5ml) twice weekly until the child is one year old. If he remains free of the above symptoms, the quantity can then be increased more rapidly over the next couple of weeks.

This means that from the second year onwards, the child will be able to have two or three cupfuls of fresh cows' milk daily. If biodynamic milk is available, or failing that, organic, then maximum life forces contained in the milk will be a source of real nourishment for the child's bodily organism. It is important to use unhomogenised milk.

Research at Fairfield University, USA, has shown a connection between homogenised milk and myocardial infarction (heart attack). (See Appendix A.) It is better to use fresh goats' milk rather than homogenised cows' milk. We must also consider sheep's milk.

## Sheep's milk

This has been shown to be less allergenic than goats' milk.[5] In the child's second year and onwards, its high protein content of 5.5% and equally high mineral content of 1% are no longer a problem. In fact, this could be useful for dreamy children reluctant to take hold of earth forces. However, sheep's milk is not readily available except in yogurt form; if it can be obtained it is thoroughly recommended.

# Goats' milk

The goat has a lively nature, not so peaceful as the cow. Its milk therefore has a different quality from cows' milk. While we cannot measure this kind of quality in the same way as the milk's chemical composition, it is nevertheless a reality which mother must consider. Its composition is much the same as cows' milk (see table for protein and mineral content in Chapter 5), but it is lacking in folic acid. However, as this is available in many foods including yeast and green leafy vegetables, a child having a normal diet would receive adequate amounts. If there is any doubt because of poor appetite etc. then folic acid supplement can be given in tablet form. It is often supposed that children who are unable to tolerate cows' milk will be able to cope with goats' milk. But research has shown this supposition to be a fallacy.[6]

# Almond milk

This is a tasty milk, easy to make, and is usually enjoyed by children. It is an excellent nutrient, but almonds are expensive, and this could exclude it as a daily family drink for some people. (To make this milk, see Appendix B.)

# Soya milk

The use of infant formula made from soya bean is now being questioned. Work on this matter has been done in New Zealand, and it has been suggested that 'it would be prudent for general sales of soy formulas to be stopped'.[7] However, it is important to state that this study was carried out on animals only. This is one of the reasons why the findings of the study have not been accepted in Australia; it has been said that there is not yet enough information to justify banning the manufacture of the product.

A section in *The Incarnating Child* examined the family of legumes to which the soya bean belongs, noting 'animal' qualities such as a high protein content, and a blood-like substance, leghaemaglobin, in the nodules of the legume root. These animal-like qualities of the soya bean have a tendency to harden the body. Dr Margarethe Hauschka advises the introduction of peas and beans into the child's diet at five years of age. She bases this on the nature of the legume. This hardening tendency coupled with the work done in New Zealand, (albeit only on animals), would surely indicate caution in the use of soya products in the child's early years.[8]

# Rice milk

The nature of rice has been set out in Appendix C. While its 'non-earthiness' could be an advantage in balancing much that today would firmly bind us to the earth, a constant intake of rice in the early years could hinder the child's growing earth consciousness. Its daily use as a milk for young children should be carefully considered.

Looked at overall, one could choose as follows for children over one year of age:

First choice – biodynamic unhomogenised fresh cows' milk.
Second choice – organic unhomogenised fresh cows' milk.
Third choice – fresh goats' milk.
Fourth choice – almond milk.
Fifth choice – soya milk or rice milk.

As stated above, sheep's milk is not readily available in all countries, therefore it is not included here.

The above choices apply to the healthy, allergy-free child. If there is any condition needing medical or homoeopathic treatment, then mother must listen carefully to professional advice and adjust the child's feeding pattern accordingly.

Weaning from the breast and choice of another milk is an important step for both mother and child. Breast milk contains the forces of mother's life, carrying her hereditary traits, and is a very special and personal gift to her child. She will want to replace it with a food which also has maximum life-forces, for it is the living quality of our food which nourishes us.

# 7

# The Rhythm of the Day

## as told by Leanne[1]

*Beloved Child, I tune you*

Leanne is a kindergarten teacher; her husband, Paulo, a doctor specializing in family medicine. Together they have worked to achieve a daily rhythm for their three children. This chapter is based on their story.

It is morning. The dawn has splashed a myriad colours across the sky, and already the sun has begun its ascent from the depths of the horizon.

In the adjacent room the three children are awake, chattering, calling for mother. It is time for everybody to get up. The children draw back the curtains to greet the day – 'Good morning, new day. Good morning, great sun'. It is a morning ritual in which mother, father and all the children participate.

Father goes off to shower and shave, and mother and children dress. Then it is breakfast time. If possible, this is a family meal to establish a feeling of belonging together. It is good to have this to carry through the day. In winter months, oatmeal porridge warms and sustains, and on hot summer days, something light nourishes. Mother prepares a school lunch, and father and Jessica set off for work and school.

Soon it is time to take Johanna to kindergarten, and after she is settled there, mother and Oliver return home. Now it is work time for mother, while Oliver follows on, 'helping' with washing, cleaning and the thousand and one other things that need to be done.

The clock says it is time to pick up Johanna. She is animated from playing with other children, has several paintings under her arm, and chatters about this and that all the way home. Oliver yawns, for it is time for lunch and then bed for the afternoon sleep. Johanna must rest too.

Lunchtime is over, the children bedded down for their afternoon rest (and hopefully, sleep!), and mother, gathering herself together, sits down with a cup of tea. This is the time of BLISS.

Soon, (so it seems) the two children are awake, have climbed out of bed, full of life, ready for action. So, the afternoon begins. There could be a shopping expedition, a visit to the beach or swimming pool, visiting friends, creative play at home, making a doll from straw or playing games.

Jessica returns home from school, brought by a friend. She says she's hungry, so there is fruit or a cookie for all. If weather permits, it is now time for outdoor activity. Jessica has been indoors most of the day, and later there could be homework.

*Singing the grace at mealtimes, holding hands. Michael and Katrina, and Julian, Nicholas and Mikhaila*

It is evening. Father has returned home, and now it is dinner time. This is always a family affair. The children have helped to set the table, and Jessica has picked fresh flowers and lit the candles. All are seated at the table, and the grace is sung, all holding hands, forming a circle. The earth and sun are thanked for their gifts of food and warmth. It is a social family gathering, sometimes with grandma and grandpa present or a special friend.

After bath and pyjamas there follows a special time. It is the going to bed ritual. Before closing the curtains, the children say Goodbye to the day. Perhaps they will wave and sing a Goodnight song; or maybe gaze in wonder at the countless stars, and ask mother if that is where the angels live. Curtains are closed, a candle lit, and children in bed. Mother or father tells a magic story. Then all say a prayer together...

As I go to sleep each night
An angel watches o'er me
And fills my soul with flooding light
And guides me to the stars so bright
And blesses me each morning.

Johanna blows out the candle (it is her turn tonight), lights are out, and mother and father leave. Then there are whisperings, confidences exchanged, cuddling up to one's favourite doll, and soon (hopefully) all is quiet.

Thus can be the rhythm of the day for persevering parents. It is not easy to achieve. It needs planning, resolution on the part of both parents, constant practice, and children who have had the blessing of firm, kindly and authoritative guidance. Then each day becomes a new experience, a new wonder. When one meets with families whose daily life unfolds in such a rhythm, one sees in the faces of the children rare qualities. It is as though a sunbeam shines through their eyes. Would that all children could have such experience!

# 8

# Our Evolving Consciousness

## Life in the 21st century

*Beloved Child, I free you*

> The old order changeth, yielding place to new,
> And God fulfills himself in many ways,
> Lest one good custom should corrupt the world.[1]

With these words Tennyson expresses the continual flux and change in the patterns of human unfolding. Rudolf Steiner dealt with the same subject in a somewhat different way in a lecture given in June 1915, in which he spoke of 'Preparing for the sixth Epoch'.[2]

While such thoughts of a deeper and broader background to life may seem remote from a mother's daily tasks, yet they relate directly to her mothering skills. For this 'preparing' that Steiner speaks of begins at birth, is guided throughout childhood and the teenage years by the parents, and then becomes the responsibility of the young adult herself.

Let us attempt to gain a clear understanding of what this means, and mother's role in such preparation. If we think in terms of preparing the child for life in the 21st century, rather than for the more remote 'sixth epoch', we will stand on more realistic ground.

Let's first take a bird's-eye view over long historical epochs, one in which we can recognize a clear progression in the evolution of human consciousness.

In ancient times we find almost no opportunity for the 'common people' to express their own individuality. In fact, ancient literature such as the Old Testament,[3] shows that for these people there was no experience of the 'I', only of belonging to a tribe or group. Intellectual faculties of questioning and seeking came much later – the questing human intellect was a priceless gift from the Greeks. Today, we use it constantly in daily life. Later still, roughly in the 15th century, came the development of scientific thought and a renaissance in art, which represented a tremendous forward stride in human consciousness. This was the beginning of an opportunity to experience oneself as an individual, of becoming conscious and self-aware as 'I'; and this intensified as human thinking developed.

We have come a long way from tribal (group) consciousness to a sense of freedom attained through one's own individual self. This progression can be summed up by saying that the right consciousness for today – and more so for tomorrow – is one which gives a sense of individuality, a sense of freedom, particularly freedom of thought. The 'I am' experience also enables us to take the next step forward to 'You are' and We are' – developing, in other words, a new sense of conscious unity with our fellow human beings.

With this picture of the pattern of our evolving consciousness, let us return to our theme of mothering, and ask what practical use this may be in a mother's daily tasks. From a certain perspective we will find that it is highly relevant. In the above mentioned lecture Rudolf Steiner speaks of the difference between the old and new consciousness, saying:

> In later years, human beings must receive new forces. The factor of blood (old force) is not meant to (i.e. cannot) encompass communities. [...] In the future the spirit will only manifest in a community where brotherhood prevails.[4]

Taking this to heart, and remembering the evolution of human consciousness as briefly outlined above, it becomes obvious that

mother has a key role in preparing humanity's future. To explore this theme let us first consider the process of freeing, a process which leads to gaining a sense of one's own self. This starts at birth, and proceeds throughout childhood, and is an essential experience for the child – enabling her, subsequently, to develop the capacity to stand as an individual in a community of free people.

# The freeing process

In the uterus the child is unfree, being totally dependent upon the mother for all sustenance. The first step in the freeing process is taken when the child emerges and takes a first breath. But an intimate connection to the mother's body is still maintained in breast feeding, and in the close bodily contact during the breastfeeding period.

Then comes weaning from the breast, a further freeing from mother's body. But the child still remains within the mother's subtle body of soul forces, the 'Madonna's Cloak' of *The Incarnating Child,*[5] sharing her soul life. This intimate soul connection remains until the birth of thinking at about age three. This has been portrayed as a withdrawing and folding back of the Madonna's Cloak. It can also be described as a stepping free of mother's body of soul forces. But a close link remains, this time in family life, which in some ways is the soul equivalent to breastfeeding on the bodily level. All the elements of soul in family life sustain the child's soul until puberty – nurturing, guiding and protecting. Then comes a dramatic change.

At puberty the teenager frees herself from family life, gaining the capacity for independent judgement and rational decision making. Whether or not she continues to live in the family home is not the vital point, so much as the seeking for freedom and independence characteristic of this time. Mother and father are no longer authorities as they had been previously. In fact they are out of touch, not 'with it'. The teenager starts making her own choices, in line with the mores of her peers rather than with family values. It is almost a 'tribal' consciousness – doing what is approved of by the peer group.

At 21 years, this changes again, for now the ego begins the task of gradually developing the soul forces laid down in childhood, and one by one, begins to penetrate the three members of the soul. This is the final freeing, the emancipating step which leads into the future.

In all we can recognize seven stages to this process, the number governing earthly human rhythms.[6] It is of utmost value to the child if each stage is experienced at the time of optimum readiness. This poses very down-to-earth questions relating to prolonged breastfeeding, and the practice of parents and children sleeping together in the family bed for a number of years. But before going on to discuss these matters, let us summarize the seven stages of freeing for the human child.

1. Birth
2. Breastfeeding (peripheral body connection)
3. Weaning from mother's breast (but remaining in her soul body)
4. The birth of thought, and stepping free of mother's soul forces
5. Family life (peripheral soul connection)
6. Puberty, the birth of independence.
7. The beginning of adulthood, as the ego begins to penetrate into the soul.

This gaining of a sense of individuality is the only basis for the future development of brotherhood, the community of free individuals of the future. It is essential for mother to fully understand this, and to be able to apply it in her mothering decisions. Let us make this more concrete by examining the two questions above – the shared family bed and prolonged breast feeding:

# The Family Bed [7]

In past centuries, it was common practice for the whole family to sleep together. Mother and father and all the children shared the same bed until the children felt ready to move out of it; and that could vary from pre-school to school age according to the family situation and the child's decision. During the 20th century this pattern changed, and it has now become common practice for each child to sleep in a separate bed, often in his or her own room, while the parents occupy the 'main bedroom'. In the last few years this practice has been called into question again, with many people reverting to what was once an accepted pattern.

To examine this trend, let us briefly restate the composite nature of the human being. There is the physical body, that can be perceived by the senses; a body of life forces; and a body of psychological (soul) forces.[8] These latter two are not sense perceptible, and therefore it is difficult for many people to readily acknowledge their existence. However, they are realities perceptible to those able to transcend the limitations of the senses and behold the non-material. It is the physical body which carries our racial characteristics – Asian people, for example, have a different body build and appearance from, say, Africans or Eskimos. In like manner, our inner characteristics are carried by our subtle bodies. For instance, our personality, desires, likes and dislikes etc, are part of our soul, while hereditary traits and more permanent characteristics such as temperament, aptitudes and so on, manifesting in behaviourial patterns throughout life, are 'housed' in our life body.

When people sleep together, an interweaving of their subtle bodies occurs: life forces carried by parents flow over and penetrate the subtle body of child or children, becoming absorbed by them into their own life body. In other words, the child receives a strong influx of hereditary forces which her own immature life body is unable to fend off. Parental characteristics, attitudes, temperament and habits invade her being, and if the process is prolonged, become permanently stamped upon her. This is a perfect preparation for group-soul (tribal) consciousness. All the mores of the folk are absorbed, become part of the child, and are carried over into adulthood. This fosters a readiness to accept current values without question, a tendency to go along with the group and rely on traditional patterns, rather than expressing one's own individuality.

These are the dangers of a child's long exposure to parental hereditary forces. But if the will is well developed and the ego strong, then these can be overcome or to some extent mitigated in later life. However, the tendency remains, and can be a hindrance to the future development of an 'I am' consciousness and a sense of individual freedom. We have seen that these latter will be essential prerequisites for community life of the future.

Those who advocate such practices do so out of a genuine desire to return to 'a more natural' life. Their fundamental error is that they look only at today's disturbed soul life, and have no awareness of the evolving human spirit. Their recommendations would return us to a consciousness suitable only for times long past.

A second error is the conviction that community life is best prepared by people who, as children, experienced a close-knit family life. While this view has much to commend it, it is only a partial truth. The real truth must be sought in the evolution of mankind, and the need for strong individuality (not individualism!). To prepare this, as we have seen, there must be a gradual process of freeing extending throughout the whole of childhood. This is the true preparation for mankind's future. Prolonged co-sleeping prepares the group-soul of yesteryear. To impose it upon a child, is, in a way, a trespass.

So is there a place at all for a child or children sleeping in the parental bed? Yes, there most certainly is!

We know from a number of studies, particularly those of Klaus and Kennell,[9] that attachment to the mother ...

> is crucial to the survival and development of the infant. [...and] perhaps the mother's attachment to her child is the strongest bond in the human.[10]

We have come to know this as 'bonding'. It occurs in what the above authors call the 'maternal sensitive period', the period immediately after birth. 'During this enigmatic period, complex interactions between mother and infant help to lock them together.' [11]

So it is absolutely essential for the newborn infant and mother to cuddle close together, touching, making eye contact, forming a bond which hopefully will endure throughout life. The most comfortable place for this to happen is in bed, for there both mother and infant can be fully relaxed, given up to each other. If the birth has taken place at home, then the parental bed is the usual choice. It is the perfect milieu for bonding with the precious new arrival.

As the weeks go by, there are a number of options for the infant's sleeping place. Some parents choose the parental bed, others a basinette or cradle next to mother's side of the bed, and others, after two or three weeks or months, move the cradle to the baby's own nursery. Which option is chosen, is, like all decisions affecting the family, a very personal one.

Eventually there comes a time when it is obvious the child is ready to take a further step towards earth consciousness. Visual and auditory sense impressions become more important, teeth begin to erupt, foods other than milk are introduced, and the child begins to be mobile on the floor. A new stage has been reached, frequently sensed intuitively by mother, as her own soul and the child's are strongly connected. This usually occurs at about 6 months of age. Some parents choose this time for 'giving the baby more space', as a number of mothers have expressed it; others wait a few weeks longer, especially if the baby is distressed by cutting teeth. It is a matter of mother feeling the time of optimum readiness for the child to vacate the parental bed. The changes should be made gradually in the following way:

**First:** Put baby in own cot, placed next to mother's side of the bed.
**Second:** Move cot (with baby!) well away from parents' bed, but leave in the same room.
**Third:** Move cot into baby's own room.

Take 7 to 10 days between each change, and if the baby becomes upset then increase the interval to 2 or 3 weeks. It is a matter of parents persevering in a loving but firm way. It must always be remembered that during the first three years of life the baby is enfolded in mother's soul forces (the Madonna's Cloak); and our soul life is not bound by laws which govern the material world – which includes our physical body. Soul forces extend beyond the limitations of space. The baby remains enfolded within the mother's soul wherever the cot is placed. It is the quality of mother's soul life that is the decisive factor here, not the placement of the cot. In fact, it can be said that sleeping in one's own cot is an early step in the freeing process.

While one cannot precisely recommend the right time to make a change, it is highly desirable that sleeping with the parents is NOT PROLONGED INTO YEARS. Of course, children love to come into Mother and father's bed for an early morning hug and cuddle, and this is a wonderful way for all to start the day. But that is different from fulltime sleeping together. As was already mentioned, the child who has been subject to the prolonged influence of hereditary forces could be at a marked disadvantage in later life. Wise mothering will avoid this.

## Weaning

Let us now look at weaning from the mother's breast. A good deal has been said about this in *The Incarnating Child*. It is therefore only necessary to emphasize that when breastfeeding extends over several years there is the same danger as outlined above. Breast milk contains an abundant supply of mother's life forces carrying her hereditary traits. If delayed weaning is coupled with extended sleeping in the parents' bed, then the child will most surely find it difficult to develop her own separate individuality as an adult.

## Life in the 21st century

Let us look again at this chapter's theme, life in the 21st century. We have explored one of its main characteristics, namely the ability to contribute in freedom to community life. We have seen that the foundation for this is the 'I am I myself' consciousness. But, what else is there to say?

In the previously mentioned lecture, given in June 1915, Rudolf Steiner listed three qualities characteristic of those who will be true representatives of the future. These are 'a certain moral quality, complete freedom of thought, and a higher form of community founded in the freedom of love among brothers'.[12] How can we develop these qualities in today's children? We are surrounded by forces that oppose the moral and the good: **hatred** expressed in war, rape, murder; **fear** which manifests subtly and is scarcely recognized – fear of death, fear of being alone, an incapacity to face oneself, fear of loss of status, and so on ad infinitum. **Doubt** also afflicts many people: scientists, academics, and the person next door – it is rife amongst us. To transform these into moral qualities seems to ask the impossible! How can we make a start?

Good quality family life, more than anything else, gives this possibility. It is within the family that the child learns, absorbing into her soul parental values, attitudes and behaviour. To prepare the moral life in one's child is to lead the moral life oneself. This means being aware of how we speak about the butcher, the baker, the candlestick maker and our mother-in-law. It means setting an example which is worthy of imitation. This 'new morality' demands most of all a strength of will, a capacity to do the good. The qualities gained in mothering, which have been discussed in chapter 3, give this strength. The new morality has many facets. It looks with compassion, not hate, it rejoices and feels gratitude for the good. It can be expressed in thoughts, feelings, words and deeds. And for the child, all of this can be learnt in good quality family life.

The second quality, freedom of thought, can only be achieved in adulthood, but it has its gestation in a family life free of dogma and prejudice. It is prepared by stories of great heroes, family conversation on a variety of topics free from criticism; it requires parental authority (but not authoritarianism!) which gives a structure to life within the family, a parental capacity to listen and guide. Within such an environment the child has opportunity to grow in freedom, to develop a creative, imaginative thought pattern which can flower into adulthood.

The third quality, participation in community life in freedom and love, asks for a sense of individuality strong enough to enable us to give freely of ourselves, offering our skills and love to the other. This, as described above, needs preparation throughout the childhood years, and calls for a mother's courage in guiding the child firmly through the freeing process.

All these things are difficult, but they are attainable today. Enlightened mothering is one way to attempt to achieve them.

# PART 2

# AND THE YEARS
# GO BY

# 9

# Mother, the Garden
# and the City

*Dearest mother, transplant me*

The previous chapter outlined the journey of humanity from the non-self to the self experience. We saw the need for a mother to have a clear grasp of what this means if she is to prepare her children in a suitable way for their life as adults in the 21st century; and how crucial it is not to confuse humanity's past with the demands of the present. Only if parents, especially the mother, are clear about this, can they contribute to the present and the future.

All of this may seem unreal to many people today. Civilization is rushing headlong into bio-technology, genetic manipulation, 'virtual reality' and similar realms that would appear to totally disregard the human being's true nature. 'Surely,' people often say, 'we must return to a past sanity, to the simple life of former times where we can live in tune with Nature. This is the sort of life we would wish for our children; it is for this that we will prepare them.' And so practices have arisen in family life today which are more suited to the past than to the present. We examined two of these in some detail in the last chapter.

To help gain a clearer understanding of the processes of human evolution, let us look at images contained in myth and symbol. For there we find expressed in simple pictorial language truths which have much to say to people of all times. Two such images are contained in the Old and New Testaments – the

Garden of Eden of Genesis[1] and The New Jerusalem of the Book of Revelations[2] – which sum up the whole journey of mankind in a wonderfully pictorial way.

*The primal state of being was heaven. And on the sixth day God created MAN. Made in the image of God, man was perfect. He embraced within him both masculine and feminine qualities.[3] There was logic and will, feeling and imagination all intertwined within his soul. God then planted a garden in heaven. It also was perfect. He put man in the garden to care for it and keep it.*

*Later, God separated feminine from masculine by creating woman. They were each given their own distinct qualities. Both now tended the garden with great happiness. Yet they were unaware that they were happy, for there was no consciousness of self, no knowledge of happiness or unhappiness. They simply lived and worked in the garden. Theirs was a state of unconscious bliss.*

*All of this changed when the wily serpent beguiled the woman. Now God banished the pair to earth, and thorns and thistles appeared and multiplied. Yet they kept in touch with heaven, and when the woman gave birth to her first child she said, 'I have gotten a man from the Lord'; and on the birth of her third child, she said, 'God hath appointed me another seed...'*

*As time went on, epoch following epoch, things became different. Woman and man lost touch with heaven, and as they did so, in corresponding measure, they came to KNOW. They came to know happiness and unhappiness; they increased in consciousness, and sought knowledge of their inward self. But often, in the depths of their soul, they yearned for the perfection of the garden.*

*Many ages later, John had a vision. It was as though an angel carried him to a high mountain, and on looking up he beheld a City resplendent with golden streets, precious gems, and perfect in every way. It seemed to John that this was Jerusalem, totally renewed. It moved down out of the clouds and came to earth. Within it, all former things were redeemed, all was transformed, fulfilled and complete.*

How are we to respond to these images? Are they relevant to our theme of mothering? Let us first turn to the City.

We can envisage that what St John describes is a picture of the city of the far distant future in which woman and man can live in happiness and knowledge, loving each other and their neighbour, giving freely of themselves to the community, doing to others as they would wish it were done to them. This is the city for which multitudes of people yearn today, but they have no idea how to find it. It is the city which today's children will seek in the years to come; and it is of urgent importance that their upbringing should enable them to develop the individual will and strength to pursue their search in freedom. This means that a mother must be fully aware of what was said in the previous chapter and recognize its immediate relevance, truly understanding the difference between the consciousness of the group soul and that of the 'I' or egohood. Moreover, she must put this understanding into practice in all matters relating to the child's care.

Let's now look more closely at these images to see what else can be learnt from them. Returning to the Garden and the young child, we see in both a state of pristine innocence; and it is within this innocent state of unconscious bliss that the young child needs to live. Only at puberty does the wily serpent intrude, and only then should the innocence give way to knowledge. Today, the garden can be planted everywhere. It is a state of soul, not a place. It can blossom in every home, pour out its radiant colours in bushland, village, town or city. We all need its beauty and lovely perfumes to refresh our soul from time to time; and children need to live fully in its protecting groves until puberty.

But as adults we must also look to the City. This also denotes a state of being and is not a place. It too is universal and can be found everywhere if one opens one's eyes and looks. The New Jerusalem is sought in many so-called 'new age' movements – environmental issues, concern and help for the needy, therapeutic work and so on. It can only be fully established by a community of free people working in harmony and love. When this happens it can also come into being in every home, in bushland, village, town or city.

While the Garden was given, planted by God, it is a human task to prepare the City. This brings us back to the mother, to her giving, receiving and encompassing work. For it is these qualities practised in her everyday life which lay enduring foundations upon which future generations will be able to build.

# 10

# Deciding

*Dearest mother, uphold me*

*Dear Child,*
*Please try to understand. I have given the matter my most penetrating*
*thought, listened as my heart pulsed anxiously, and tried to still my*
*turbulent emotions. Please listen carefully and I will explain. I have*
*decided to take part-time work away from home; just one or two days a*
*week at first until we see how things turn out. We desperately need extra*
*money to save for your schooling. It seems the only way...Your care?...*
*We will arrange the very best possible.*

The time often comes today when women decide to add work
outside their home to their mothering career. This decision affects
both their feeling and thinking life. There are many reasons for it.
Let us explore it further.

To understand this from a mother's point of view, we need a
picture of what is happening in her soul.[1] During pregnancy, all
through the breastfeeding period and until the child has reached
age three, a mother lives strongly in her feelings. During this period
many women find they are unable to concentrate their thoughts,
and feel they have lost a former capacity for clarity of thinking.
This often occurs during the early or mid twenties. By the end of
the twenties, say at about 28 years of age, or the early thirties, the
ego begins to enter the rational mind, developing what had
previously been laid down, and learning to use it more and more.
Now bringing with them a greatly enhanced feeling life, mothers
begin to look outward as their intellect demands further challenge.

This challenge can often be met in activities associated with family life. For instance, mother might find herself a pillar of the kindergarten or school committee, organizing fund-raising activities, giving lectures, arranging seminars and all the myriad activities associated with the children's school years. All of this needs a well-developed will directed by clear thinking, and warmed by heart forces. Here mother needs all the skills she has developed in earlier years. It is a further step in her mothering career, part of her full-time mothering vocation. However, for some mothers, employment in the 'outside world' better fulfils this need for intellectual challenge. It is a very personal matter. We are speaking here of mothers whose children attend kindergarten or are at school.

Other mothers today find full-time mothering unsuited to their personal needs. They feel unable to find satisfaction in this way. These are often professional or business women who wish to continue their work in the outside world. If this can be arranged on a part-time basis for the first few years, the breastfeeding time completed, and high quality continuity of home care be provided, (such as grandma or a permanent nanny), then home and outside work become dual careers. This gives some women the satisfaction they seek. Such responsible choice must be respected. It is in no way superior or inferior to mothering as a full-time vocation; but it is different.

For others there are pressing financial needs which demand that mother contribute to the family income. But it is essential that breastfeeding is not jeopardised and that a mother makes the best arrangements available for the care of the child. Family day-care is often a solution in these circumstances. One must also consider the age of the child/children in making choices.

The single mother is in much the same position, and often needs to earn a salary to survive. Yet many single mothers, especially those prepared to live simply, are able to 'get by' doing a few odd jobs here and there – e.g. house cleaning, ironing, or even gardening and lawn mowing.

And there are mothers who choose to do two or three days of outside work per week to 'keep their hand in' and not get left behind in their sphere of work. This can apply to nurses, teachers, social workers, and a host of others in a variety of occupations. Here it is not so much a matter of earning money but of keeping up to date. Again, the age of the child/children and the care available are of prime importance.

Role swapping, or sharing the care with father is a fairly recent phenomenon, often undertaken out of financial necessity, or for any number of other reasons. It can be done either full-time or part-time according to parents' choice.

Then there is the woman who chooses not to breastfeed and who returns to full-time outside work a few weeks after the baby's birth, placing the infant in a full-time day-care centre. One questions whether this is mothering at all! Perhaps 'woman with child' would be a more apt description. Two world authorities on the care and upbringing of children, Penelope Leach and Steve Biddulph have much to say about this in their respective books, *Children First*,[2] and *More Secrets of Happy Children*.[3] The former calls a chapter on this subject 'Day Care: Dreams and Nightmares'; and in chapter four of Steve Biddulph's book, he says,

> It is my belief that long day-care of children under three, in an institutional setting like a creche, will result in those children having a seriously deprived childhood experience.

No further comment is needed!

So what is the ideal time for mother to begin outside work, and what are the ideal arrangements that must be made if the child or children are not to be at a disadvantage? These are tremendously important questions, and to answer them we must now look at the developing child.[4]

During the first seven years of life, the ego is engaged in building the child's physical body. To lay foundations that will endure throughout life, there is a need for unpolluted food (preferably bio-dynamic or organic), good quality sense impressions,

warm clothing, adequate rest and so on. Mother is the best one to
ensure that these needs are met. During this time the 'life body' is
going through its gestation period, and its subsequent healthy
vigour or otherwise depends upon the quality of the child's
experiences during this time. The life body (or one could say the
'health body' carrying the immune system) is 'born' at age seven,
and then becomes the focus of the ego's activity. It is also built up
and nourished by good quality food, experiences in natural
surroundings (camping, trekking etc.), artistic pursuits, imaginative stories, and a healthy rhythmic lifestyle. A similar process
takes place at puberty when soul forces are released. These also
can be thought of as constituting a 'soul body' needing nurture
and direction.

Accompanying these three 'births' is a soul development.[5] In
the first period the child's active play lays foundations for a later
strong will capacity; in the second period, rhythms and participation in the arts stir the child's feeling life; and at puberty,
intellectual thinking comes into its own.

This picture of the various processes taking place within the
mother and the child, puts us in a better position to attempt to
answer our previous questions – What is the ideal time for mother
to take up a former career, and what are the ideal arrangements
that will ensure the maintenance of family life?

There is no simple answer, for these are largely individual
matters. But the wisdom of Solomon, set out in the Book of
Ecclesiastes,[6] can be a help:

> To everything there is a season and a time to every
> purpose under the heaven: a time to be born and a time to
> die; ... a time to weep and a time to laugh; ... a time to
> embrace and a time to refrain from embracing; ...

Therefore there must also, presumably, be a time for mothering.
Joseph Chilton Pearce, a well known researcher into child
development, and author of a number of books on this subject, has
much to say that is enlightening. He bases his viewpoint partly on
the growth and development of the senses and neurological

system, and partly on his own observations. In his book, *The Magical Child*,[7] he speaks of functions of the brain being undifferentiated during the first three years, and not until after the age of seven do areas of the brain begin to specialize. It is only then that 'the social self becomes fully functional ...'[8]

This would seem to indicate that only at about age seven can a child really relate to people outside the immediate family.

Differentiating between the roles of father and mother, Pearce says, 'Nature has designed it so that mother is matrix ...' He describes father's role as forming a bridge from mother to the outside world, and then 'to the larger world of society ...' This process starts 'somewhere in the second year of life',[9] and goes on to age seven. Then father 'is the pull to the unknown; the mother is the known, the touchstone. In balance and harmony they provide the perfect ground for growth.' He then makes a most significant statement: 'Therefore, I will refer from now on to parent or parents rather than to just mother.'[10]

We see then, according to the above research, that seven years is an age of transition from mother, the former matrix of life, to parents and the 'larger world of society'. Only then can the brain specialize and 'the social self become fully functional'. This indeed brings great illumination to our question, 'What is the mothering period?' The answer can only be that mother is the king-pin (or queen-pin), the matrix, from conception to age seven. This is specifically the mothering time. To speak of parenting during this time is an untruth. Father has, of course, been greatly involved during this period, but not until the child's second year does his specific task start. Then he begins to form a bridge to the outside world, and this process finds its culmination when the child is seven. This is the age, as I have mentioned, when the child's physical body has been built up, and the life body released. The child is now at a new stage of development, with the ego's work on the physical body (which includes the brain) completed. Here before us, then, we have a clear, research-substantiated picture of the mothering period before it transforms into the next stage of 'parenting'.

To return to our original question, what then is the ideal time for mother to move on to a sphere of work outside the family? Does knowledge of a specific mothering time answer this question? Our reply must be, 'Partially, yes...'

If all conditions are ideal, economically sound, mother finding her career at home fully satisfying, father supportive, children stable, family life established, then when the youngest child has reached the age of seven, this would seem to be the ideal time for mother to 'move on' should she so choose. By then it is likely that she has recaptured the ability to think clearly, and her imagination has become active. In a family of three children, the specific mothering period would then extend over approximately 12-14 years depending on how the children were spaced. If there were two children, the period would naturally be shorter – say 9 or 10 years. If we agree that an average adult working life is roughly forty years, it will become clear that mothering occupies a comparatively short time-slot within the whole of life. For that reason also, it must be cherished.

But life in today's world is very often far from ideal. Money may be urgently needed for any number of reasons; there is the spectre of broken relationships, single mothers coping on their own, and all the other potential difficulties that can arise. Such situations demand choices that are far from ideal. How can reality and ideals be reconciled?

The choice, let us emphasize once more, can only be the mother's or parents'; and it needs to be a conscious one, based on an overall view of the situation. When choices are made responsibly (the key word here) and not out of selfishness or simply by caving in to outside pressures, then they should naturally be respected. We must recognize that human beings are diverse creatures, each with an individual karmic pattern which can only be fulfilled in an individual way. However, whatever the situation, there are a few crucial matters which should under no circumstances be compromised. One of these is breastfeeding. To wean an infant in the first few weeks of life and return to full-time work is really not mothering, whatever the financial pressures or other difficulties. Equally disastrous for the child's spiritual and social development, and therefore subsequent wellbeing, is an ever-changing pattern of child care and minders while mother is at full-time work. The more the minding situation is stable and resembles home life (rather than an institution) the better it will probably be – depending, of course, on the personality and kindliness of the minder.

So even though the *ideal* time for a mother to seek outside work is when the youngest child has reached age seven, there *are* alternative, compromise times if the need is pressing and the situation becoming desperate. We have seen that at three years of age the child separates from the mother's soul life and recognises himself as 'I'.[11] This is a time when the child asks constant questions about the world and life, for the world begins to look different as the Madonna's cloak gradually withdraws and the child sees the world through his own eyes instead of through mother's as previously. This can be a time of anxiety for a child, and he needs mother's presence and reassurance. But after another three to six months or so, when the child is possibly at kindergarten, mother may safely consider part-time work. Anything earlier than this could be fraught with future difficulties for the child, depending on arrangements made for care, and how long mother is away. But if care arrangements are 100% satisfactory and a child seems happy during the mother's absence, then many mothers choose to do a few hours of outside work each week when the little one is about two years of age. In these circumstances, it is helpful if there is an older sibling too, so the young one doesn't feel all alone.

We must now look at possible solutions for childcare should a mother choose to do some 'outside' work for whatever reason. Home care by a 'nanny' can be arranged while mother works part-time; and in the case of an infant, if home and work place are near each other, then the baby can be taken to his mother for cuddling and breast feeding at intervals during the day. Sometimes father or grandmother will be the carer while mother does a few hours evening work. Then expressed breast milk can be left at home in case of emergency so that breastfeeding is not interrupted, and the child remains in his own home with a familiar person. Swapping child-minding with a friend on a weekly basis can also work well, and gives each party one day off a week or fortnight according to arrangements. Again, this should only take place after the child or children are weaned. For older children it is essential that there be somebody familiar to welcome them home from school, and remain with them until a parent returns.

In all these cases, and in fact, generally, it is a great help for the children if family life is rich and active. For instance, the evening dinner can be made a festival with candles, a thanksgiving for the food, and family conversation; picnics, visits to friends, celebrations of birthdays and seasonal festivals etc, give children an environment within which each can contribute in an individual way while feeling firmly rooted in family life. To provide this environment becomes one of the many tasks of responsible mothering and parenting.

*Katrina and children playing games after the birthday meal.*

In all that has been said a most important factor plays its part. Although our age has tended to blur the differences and distinctions between male and female, for all sorts of 'politically correct' reasons, it is nevertheless vital to understand how the human soul expresses itself through a female body on the one

*Christmas dinner celebration. Paul, Jenny, Jesse and Raina*

hand, and a male body on the other. Three main functions or aspects of the soul are those of thinking, feeling and willing. When housed in a male body, the soul has the opportunity to develop its will and logical thinking functions; and when in a female body, those of feeling and imaginative thinking. As life follows life the human soul has the opportunity to develop in a balanced way, to experience first one set of soul qualities then another.[12]

The mothering period gives a wonderful opportunity to enhance the feminine qualities of feeling and imagination. And when father shares the caring as most fathers do today, then he must also draw upon his feminine qualities of soul. He too must express tenderness in his activities, gentleness of speech, tell the story imaginatively and from his heart. These are the mothering qualities, which father's soul also contains. During the child's early years he must learn to express them through his masculine body, becoming, transitionally, a kind of 'second mother'.

When the child reaches about seven years of age, then, as I have mentioned, parenting begins. Now a father starts to draw on his masculine soul qualities while a mother continues to express her feminine side. Thus the child is nurtured harmoniously and his soul qualities come into balance. At 21 years the soul is penetrated by ego forces, and the young adult must now find an

individual direction. But this is only possible if, from puberty to
emerging adulthood, the soul has received the firm guidance and
authority inherent in the masculine. This is largely father's
responsibility. But mother must also use these qualities, build a
framework and boundaries, and work with the child's growing
logical thinking. It is a real challenge to her feminine body, but
one her soul can readily encompass once she understands its
necessity. At this stage we must speak of 'fathering' as the
dominant soul quality practised by both parents.

Finally, we come to recognise that mothering makes possible
the growth of much that is otherwise neglected in our techno-
logical age. Today's economic aspirations, ambitions and
materialistic ways of thought do little to enrich the human soul
and spirit, whereas the vocation of mothering (often regarded as
an unrealistic ideal) truly feeds and nurtures it. Mothering as a
vocation is not an impossible ideal in today's world, but an actual
and attainable reality. In fact, skilled mothering makes the
impossible possible. This is a miracle, usually unrecognized and
unsung.

# 11

# Creches, Care-givers and Controversy

*Dearest mother, protect me*

In view of issues explored in the previous chapter, let us now examine current research into day-care centres. This will beg the question whether common-sense has any place at all in making decisions nowadays, or whether the dictates of 'science' are the only decisive ones. Another vital question, as we consider the mother's role in the late 20th century, is 'What is freedom?'

In the January-February 1996 issue of *Quadrant*,[1] there is an article by a Melbourne writer, Anne Manne, headed 'Electing a New Child'. She describes this new child as 'independent and competent, (one) whose qualities dovetail nicely with the needs of adults to be free'. One assumes, in the context of the article, that this freedom is the opportunity to be free *from* family life and the upbringing of the child/children. Anne Manne comments on this idea of today's child thus:

> It is distinctive of our age to be enthusiastic about early independence and competence. These traits in the child obviously release the mother from the traditional role of mothering, thus leading to the above so-called 'freedom'.

Anne Manne then goes on to question the validity of this viewpoint, and in doing so explores the research and reported conclusions of many working in this field. She particularly questions the claims of a senior member in the Australian Institute of Family Studies, Dr. Ochiltree, who argues (in two recently published papers) that her survey of 'forty years research reveals no problems with childcare as long as it is of good quality'; that 'Australian childcare is generally of high quality'; and thirdly, that 'overseas there is a hegemony of approving opinion in social science supporting institutional care for the youngest age groups'.

This leads on to a fascinating and revealing exploration of the work of overseas psychologists and research social scientists. We learn of the work of the American Edward Zigler, an 'eminent developmental psychologist', of Jay Belsky, also an American development psychologist, of Alan Sroufe's Minnesota studies, the claims of Alison Clarke Stewart who 're-interpreted the data concerning 'non-compliance' and aggression as a form of enhanced social competence, a modern and desirable kind of assertiveness', (this was emphatically countered by Belsky); we hear of Professor Jerome Bruner of Oxford whose qualitative research concentrated on the child's experience while in childcare rather than on the measuring of long-term effects. ('He reveals a world of the child at the minder's and at day-nurseries which is deeply disquieting...'); and we learn of the work of Andersson from Sweden 'which indicated not problems but benefits from childcare'.

So we have the most diverse conclusions from overseas research, certainly not 'a hegemony of approving opinion'. In fact, the work of these skilled researchers presents a picture of uncertainty, of questioning, and in some cases a willingness to explore possible harmful effects of long-term exposure to creche and other forms of child care for the very young. This possible harmfulness, we learn, can take the form of aggression, withdrawal, learning difficulties, an incapacity to relate to others, etc. These effects are then interpreted in a variety of ways by individual researchers – e.g. Alison Clarke Stewart on the one hand, and Belsky on the other.

Scientific research, however, is not the only way of arriving at the truth. There is also commonsense. The former needs an ability for observation, a well developed intellect with its capacity for logical deduction. It operates in the realm of quantity and measurement, and the truth it (hopefully) discovers tends to be of a measurable kind. Commonsense, on the other hand, can be described as a combination of knowing, intelligence, feelings and a practicality which, together, lead to the formation of sound judgement. A person using commonsense may or may not be highly developed intellectually.

Both of these are valid tools for the seeking human being. The former is used extensively today by research scientists, the latter by those who engage their whole being (that is, feeling and an intuitive sensing as well as thinking) in arriving at decisions. Unfortunately, the latter method is not generally recognised as reliable in determining the truth about anything. If considered at all, commonsense is regarded as 'unscientific' and therefore relegated to the dust-bin as a method of investigation. Yet it is a faculty of inestimable value to those whose heart qualities are active, who are intelligent and able to sense life's deeper meanings. As has often been stated in this book, the vocation of mothering activates and develops these qualities.

It is through commonsense that mothers know the importance of caring for their own child, of breastfeeding, of loving, and of en-joy-ing family life. Scientific research may 'prove' this or that, but the woman who *knows* has little or no need of it. Her commonsense tells her what is true for herself, the child and the family, and she makes her decisions accordingly. She has gone beyond using the intellect only, and has learnt to use her whole being.

In this context of women wanting to be free, to have opportunity to make free choices, one may well ask: What IS freedom? And why is it thought to be more attainable for, say an employee in an office (or anywhere else, for that matter) than in one's own home?

Freedom can be defined in any number of ways. It is an inner state, and has very little, if anything, to do with one's outer situation. To attain it demands constant inner striving. By striving to achieve it we can develop a capacity to obey the call of what we perceive to be the Good and the True. The task, whatever and wherever it be, is then freely accepted and undertaken with love. From this perspective, freedom is not something gained by putting one's baby in a creche.

Anne Manne's most interesting and thoughtful article just hints at these deeper issues. She speaks of the things she valued as a mother:

> ...the importance of giving children a love of the world, a sense of trust or faith which might come from the faithfulness of adults, a way of seeing and illuminating the world, a sense of being...

These values cannot be quantified or measured. Neither are they gained by outer action. They are of the nature of goodness and truth, and as such belong to our inner life.

# 12

# Brett – Man and Woman [1]

## Dearest mother, understand me

Brett is having a conversation with his mother. He is 24 years of age, has a degree in sociology and psychology, and has grown up in a stable family with mother, father and an older sister. He would seem to have had all advantages necessary to give him a firm footing in life. Yet Brett's understanding of the masculine role in today's society is confused, and this presents something of a dilemma in how he behaves towards his feminine friends. He has been called sexist when he opened the car door for a female friend, and uncouth when he has not done so. He is typical of many young men today. 'Is there a norm at all?' they ask.

The conversation turned to mothers, and Brett's conviction that he could undertake a mothering role just as well as a female. Sure, the male and female bodies are different, but so what? Once the child is weaned from the breast, then does it really matter which parent does the caring? Roles were changing, and young women these days had usurped much that had hitherto been male prerogatives. The male was no longer necessarily the sole or even the main provider, out there in the world while mother stayed at home at the kitchen stove, surrounded by nappies. 'And so,' said Brett, 'can one even speak of role swapping if there is now no such thing as a male or female role? And is there such a thing as 'mothering' at all, or should we speak of 'caring'?'

What are we to think of these attitudes, so prevalent today and so strongly experienced by many young adults, both male and female? In view of what has been said in previous chapters, it is vital that we come to some understanding of such a strong trend, expressed with such great conviction.

This question can best be understood if we look back to the Garden and forward to the City as described in chapter 9. For it is a question concerned with the human soul and its archetypal functions.

We have seen that the primal human being was both male and female. This is clearly stated in the Genesis creation story, in chapter 1, verse 27, and again in chapter 5, verses 1 and 2. Emil Bock,[2] in his book *Genesis*,[3] writes: 'The Bible says that the primordial image of the human form was hermaphroditic, combining both sexes.' The soul of this original being (called Adam in *Genesis*) was pure and whole. One could describe it as a soul composed of pure love,[4] made in the image of God. One sees this same phenomenon in most plants. They contain both male and female within the blossom. And because the plant has no soul, there is no need for differentiation of the sexes. The plant pours out its colour and perfume as a gift for all people. It neither favours nor disfavours.

However, once soul evolved (in animals and humans), then its differentiation into male and female qualities made possible a higher development. And this was necessary to enable evolution to continue. If it had not happened, we would have remained pure, innocent and unconscious, like the plants. A differentiated soul was a step forward in human evolution.

In the archetypal male we see strength, forcefulness, will, logic and so on; in the female, tenderness, gentleness, caring, imaginative thinking. These archetypal qualities are today expressed in a variety of ways. It can be said that feminism truly started with Eve. Then the soul lost its purity and its oneness, and ever since has consciously or unconsciously sought its original pure and complete state, but at a higher level. In feminism today there is a strong, usually unconscious search for the whole, an attempt to find and to share with men the original masculine-feminine soul state. That is, to recapture love in its primal pure form, free of the dualities of desire.

Only in the City, the New Jerusalem, will it be possible for this wholeness and sacrificial love to be achieved, in a synthesis of male-female qualities.[5] This is a scarcely comprehensible thought, but one we should take seriously if we are to gain any understanding of current trends exemplified by people like Brett. We must try to envisage this future male-female human being as encompassing all soul qualities, able to express masculine and feminine aspects equally well. Whether such a soul life will again need a hermaphroditic form is a matter for spiritual scientific research.

Here then, perhaps, is the distant solution of the masculine-feminine question. It can only be achieved by a love able to sacrifice itself for the good of the other, to pour out blessings for the good of the whole. Today we can only strive towards it. There are any number of paths, of which mothering is one. Feminism can be another if it can develop sacrificing love.

For something new to emerge in human evolution, there must be a very long preparation.[6] There is no such thing as instant cosmic-spiritual transformation. Such preparation is hardly discernible to begin with – we are usually entirely unsuspecting that something new could be dawning in our midst. It first appears as a minute seed, so small that we are unable to detect it. Could this be the cause of some of the contemporary mothering practices outlined in Chapter 10? Are mothers striving to be both female and male?

In that chapter we described the mother who wishes to pursue her professional or business interests as well as mothering. She feels that she needs this dual career to achieve a sense of fulfilment. Then there is the mother who wishes to do a few hours work each week to keep up to date in her work area, or the one who chooses work outside the home after the mothering period has run its course; there is also role swapping and the single mother who becomes both mother and father. These various forms of mothering are common practice today. Do they have a deeper meaning, or are they merely an expression of the times we live in: a passing phase, or an aberrant form of mothering?

Such questions are difficult to answer, but they can be looked at in another way, which may be illuminating: and that is to come to an understanding of the word 'man'.

Over the past several years the use of this word has been widely rejected, and in its place the words 'human being' or 'person' are commonly used. Thus we have 'Chairperson', not 'Chairman'; 'human beings', in preference to 'mankind', and so on.

What are we to make of this? Does it reflect the triumph of feminism, or indicate a total lack of knowledge of philology – or both?

'Man' is usually regarded as the masculine gender in contrast to 'woman', the feminine gender. Yet, in its origin, 'man' had nothing whatever to do with gender. It originated from a Sanskrit word meaning 'the thinker', and therefore can be used for either gender – both masculine and feminine.

In his published lectures on The Science of Language, given to members of the University of Oxford in 1860, the eminent scholar, Max Müller (Professor of Comparative Philology) examines, among other things, the origin of words. He says

> ...if we examine the structure of modern languages, we find that they were built up with the materials taken from the ruins of ancient languages, and every word, if properly examined, displays the visible stamp impressed upon it...by the founders...[7]

Regarding the origin and meaning of the word 'man', Müller looks not only to Greek and Latin, but also to Sanskrit. Speaking of Sanskrit, he says:

> The name, man, means simply the thinker...Man, a derivative root, means to think. From this we have the Sanskrit manu, originally meaning thinker, and then man.[8]

One could add many other examples. For instance, *manager* (the thinker who directs an activity); *Manichaean* and *Mandaean*, two early sects of educated Initiates;[9] Chairman, the thinker, be it male or female, who sits on the chair and conducts the meeting, while those perhaps less capable of thinking sat on the bench or the floor; *Mandamus,* a legal term meaning to command, or a prerogative order from a superior court to a lower tribunal; and two Sanskrit words found in Hinduism, *Brahman* and *Atman.* The former indicates a member of the highest priestly caste, often a high official in the service of the king; and the latter, the breath, refers to a metaphysical being in man which was said to be the thinker of his thoughts. All of these words indicate the original meaning of the word 'man' as one capable of reflective and creative thinking, irrespective of gender.

In contrast, the term *human* refers to our body only – the humus, or our 'humble' aspect. And in olden days, the word 'humours' was used to describe bodily fluids, bile, blood, phlegm etc. which, it was said, led to our bodily disposition, influencing our emotional life. Therefore the term 'human' does not indicate our real being, that which places us above all other creatures on earth.

Man is the only earthly being who has a reflective thinking faculty through which s/he is able to come to self-knowledge and awareness of the spirit underlying our universe. Our humus is certainly not capable of this. In fact, it perishes and returns to earth from whence it came.

In the above sense, therefore, mother and father are both 'man' (or, one could say wo-man and man, both thinkers).

The wholesale rejection of the word 'man' does nothing to solve the male/female issue. In fact, it only confuses it! Such misinterpretation debases the word's true meaning. For mother and father are not merely 'persons', and are certainly much more than bodily humus. Their real being expresses itself through the individual, reflective, cooperating thinking nature of each.

If we add this understanding to what is to become possible in The New Jerusalem, then we can come to recognise man the thinker within us, and man the self-sacrificing lover.

The world has many Bretts; and there will be more and more to come as the years go by. They question, they explore, they seek

*Mothering*

the new, and they strive to understand all issues of life. One of these issues is mothering. We welcome their questions and respect their striving. They will be the parents of tomorrow. We greet them with warmth and wish them well. Who knows what they will bring to the future!

But for the time being let us return to the solid ground of mothering as a vocation. This gives women today a certainty of heart experience. Here there is no doubt, no conjecture or fantasy. Mothering at this level is real for today; it is relevant NOW.

# 13

# Mother and the Growth of Love

*Dearest mother, meet me*

Let us speak of love, that most enigmatic of the human passions. It encompasses a wide range of the soul's feelings, from the most primitive instinctual desires to the loftiest capacity for renunciation and sacrifice. In between the former and the latter are a number of stages encompassing both the anguish of thwarted desire, and ecstatic joy in truly meeting the being of the other.

Where can mother-love be placed amidst this kaleidoscope of devotion, passion and sacrifice? Can a specific place be pin-pointed to which it essentially belongs?

To attempt to answer this question we must first explore the nature and growth of love:

First comes the physical stage, when the physical presence of the beloved is sought. Here we are in the realm of warmth. It can express itself in a naive and innocent way, for example, holding hands, or also in sexual meeting.

This can lead to devotion for the other, and usually associated with this are lunar forces of passion and desire. But there is also the happiness of doing things together, sharing secrets, sharing passions. Love at this stage is full of tenderness, and at the same time there are strong desires to belong, to be together, often to possess. It is the stage of romantic love, and is right and proper throughout the twenties and up to about the mid-thirties.

Then can come a higher stage, a recognition of the 'I' of the other; and this gives the possibility for a true human meeting, an ego to ego relationship. Former strong instinctual forces become

*Stephen and Deanne – devotion for each other*

tempered by an increasing consciousness and a certain maturation of soul. Lunar forces recede as the being of the other reveals itself more and more. It is as though light from the sun streamed into the earth, illuminating, uplifting, revealing the beauty of all things. Now comes the possibility of fully and consciously using the powers of the soul, of finding direction and purpose in life; and this leads on to still higher stages.

These higher stages of love are a transformation of the lower three, those of passion, devotion and physical warmth. Passion gives way to compassion. Desires are tamed and transformed, and healing on all levels becomes possible. These forces are transformed to become spiritualized life forces. Now there is the possibility for redemption, for new patterns of life, and within the soul, beauty at a higher level reveals itself. Love now has a transformed Venus quality: two souls meeting in desire-free devotion and in freedom.

Finally, there develops a capacity for renunciation and sacrifice. This, the free choice to renounce one's love, to sacrifice oneself for the Good, is the highest form of human love. Its most exalted expression was at Golgotha 2000 years ago. Goethe attained this sacrificial love in his seventies. The fountains of love had poured out their abundance throughout this great man's life, and he had drunk deep of their elixir. In his latter years he was able to renounce and redeem the quality of physical-warmth and contact, and achieve a selfless awareness of I-You, thus raising love into the sphere of spirit – possibly one of his greatest achievements.

Love, then, can live on many levels. It can be expressed between two individuals, or expand to a universalism. A common example of early stages of the former is romantic love. The latter is exemplified by St Francis of Assisi. 'Brother Ant' was dear to his heart – a matter of going beyond the individual and achieving a state of being which encompasses the All. It can only take place in freedom.

*Nell – friend Puss is close to her heart*

In all, this gives us seven stages of love which can be related to both human and cosmic development. How far we are able to follow this most demanding path is an individual affair, dependent largely on our personal stage of soul growth and capacity for striving. It is an arduous journey.

But now let's return to our original question: Where are we to place mother-love on this journey of the soul? This is difficult to answer, for there seems no one place we can point to. Could it be that mother-love contains the inherent possibility of proceeding through all stages of love?

The growth of mother-love can be seen during the child's early years, and can be observed developing and extending throughout the whole of life. We'll look at the early years first.

Breastfeeding encompasses the first three stages of love: the warmth of body contact, the mother's devotion to the child, and an intense emotional relationship of shared smiles, caresses and so on. Then comes the child's recognition of herself, that can be summed up as 'I am separate from You'. This occurs usually at about 2¹/2 to 3 years of age. It is associated with the birth of thinking. Now there is opportunity to meet the child rationally, to approach her through her manifest 'I'.

There follows a slight loosening of ties for both mother and child as the latter begins to walk across the bridge that leads to the outside world. Kindergarten years follow and relationships alter and transform. At school age the mother 'sacrifices' her daily care of the child, and places this in the hands of the school teacher. For close-knit families, this is often accompanied by a sense of loss on the one hand, and on the other a recognition that love demands this action.[1]

Such a picture of a love relationship between mother and child, extending through the early years of the child's life, is a microcosm of the early stages of human love in general: cuddling-up, sitting on mother's knee, fondling etc. When the child reaches puberty the third stage comes into view. Now mother and father are often seen by the teenager as restrictive, arguments ensue, passions flare, yet underneath it all there is a sense of belonging together, however tenuous this may become.

As the child grows into an adult, and the ego begins to penetrate and use the powers and capacities of the soul, a meeting at ego level can develop: mother and erstwhile child recognize each other, each as an individual. It is an 'I' to 'I' relationship in freedom.

Higher stages lead to a recognition of the other's being, of the 'You', and love is expressed in caring companionship, in identifying with the needs of the other. Gradually, 'We are' becomes attainable, and finally, mother's capacity to 'let go' at all levels.

These last three stages call for maturity of both parties. While this is often not attained, yet it is possible. When achieved, life is enhanced beyond all measure. Love is then a precious gift one to the other, a radiant jewel, illuminating, warming, and bestowing new life.

Thus it will be seen that mother-love does indeed give endless possibilities for inner growth. It is able to overcome feelings of soul emptiness and isolation, and leads to a sense of real purpose in life. This in turn gives the possibility of recognizing that the mother on earth can become a manifestation of the Divine Mother, and her daily work in the home an expression of Divine Purpose.

Thus it is possible for a mother to reach an understanding of the exalted nature of her mothering work.

# 14

# Grandmother

## The banquet of the soul

*Dearest mother, know me*

Mother has become a grandmother. Her mothering days are over. Her path through life has led along highways and low-ways, through plateaux where the sun shone, and deep dark valleys, shrouded, full of mysterious depths formerly unsuspected. She has laughed, danced, wept and despaired; lingered here to taste the luscious fruits, hastened past there, at times trembling. Mother has grown inwardly. She has learned resolution and tolerance, and developed a thousand skills and qualities which have preserved her sanity in times of stress.

She now often experiences an unexpected peace and quietness of soul; and at other times turmoil still as she observes the struggles of her adult children. She would like to help, and often does. But she knows that fundamentally they must face the fires of life themselves if they are to grow. As they matured, she attempted to meet them freely, recognizing their different individualities. And through this there developed a mutual giving and receiving, an admiration, respect and love. This was a golden crown, a holy gift, a true banquet for her soul.

She was in her mid-twenties when she first became a mother. It was a time for intense experience as she sensed her way into her new role, usually too busy to reflect upon where her path was leading. She met each day as it came, sometimes calmly, sometimes in tumult, and occasionally fear surfaced from the darker corners of life. When her second child came a few years later, she was overjoyed. Now in her late twenties, she was more confident, and seeking intellectual stimulation. She joined the kindergarten committee, helped organize functions, edited the quarterly newsletter, and entered fully into a community life connected with her mothering. The home and family remained her anchor.

As she entered her mid to late thirties, a new power seemed to enter her soul;[1] and as this grew in strength she found she began to *know*. Formerly, things had to be weighed up, worked out, statistics studied to come to an understanding of any particular situation. Now these methods started to seem far less relevant, for answers appeared almost palpably before her. She had learnt to use her soul powers cognitively.

Time went on and the forties enfolded her. Children were all at school, and now she felt an urge to enter the world of outside work. She had much to offer. Because she had learnt to direct and use her soul powers, she was no longer a slave to former extravagances of thought, and wild and frantic urges for exciting action. She was fully in charge of her inner life, and what she offered carried the stamp of her own individuality. From now on, her deeds, thoughts and words were an expression of her deeper self.

Between 42 and 49 she felt a need for re-assessment, and it was then that she made profound changes in her life. It seemed to her that planetary influences were playing strongly into her soul during this time.[2] Mars urged her on sternly, Jupiter promised wisdom as she entered her fifties. When the menopause came, she experienced it as a freeing to be no longer driven by urgent desires of body and soul, sexual or otherwise. She was now able to love without complication. It was an enormous relief. Yet she recognized that she had not truly overcome the lunar forces which had often previously overpowered her. Their compelling power had simply abated somewhat. She was immensely grateful. New friendships blossomed and former ones grew and deepened. She was able to meet the individual being of the other. The seductive flutes and harps of her younger days played a new harmonious song. She joyfully accepted the invitation to the dance.

She came to regard the menopause as one of God's great gifts to women, a signpost pointing the way ahead to new chapters of life. So mother became grandmother. Her journey continued, but now with the profound difference that she felt an unfettered freedom, being less influenced by planetary rhythms;[3] It was as though her soul feasted freely upon the sweetmeats of life. She was now in her sixties, and able to explore vast fields of inner awakening.[4] Boundless vistas lay ahead, continually beckoning her onward. She opened her hands, and many gifts came. She began to think of her next life, and of the friends she had made in this. She thought of her karmic path, and wondered what the future held. The weaving of her karma had produced a diversity of pattern – some of which was knotted and tangled, and needing to be unravelled. She now knew that life's experiences make this possible, and in the grandmothering years,[5] especially those after age 63, new karma can be consciously built, and preparations made which will carry into future lives. Thus grandmother actively prepared her future. Her latter years offered untold opportunities. She knew that it was her responsibility to grasp them, and weave into her destiny a golden thread for tomorrow.

*Mother has progressed to Grandmother. Annie, Georgia*
*and Jack with grandmother, mother and father*

# 15

# The Bell Tolls

## Mysteries of the Spirit[1]

*Dearest mother, thankyou*

It was a bright spring day when the bell tolled. The sun shone, the prunus was in bloom, and daffodils opened their golden flowers to the pervading warmth.

She was glad to cast off her earthly body. It was worn out, could no longer be repaired. Yet she felt gratitude towards it, for it had served her well, especially in her mothering years. In the panorama of her life spread out before her, she once more saw her breastfeeding days. What a joy these times had been!

She beheld the journey of her entire life – a revelation in vivid images. Soon a new journey would begin. She clutched a precious 'parcel' containing her accumulated karma. It was too cumbersome to take with her. She would deposit it for safe-keeping until her return.

When the panorama faded she found herself travelling backwards through her earthly experiences. She saw things much more clearly now, and regretted the mistakes she had made. When she came to earth again, there would be much to repair. She shuddered as she beheld her excessive mourning after her husband's death. She saw how this had, to some extent, impeded his further path. She would need repair work here.

As she proceeded backwards and relived her mothering years, she recognized that this had been her greatest fulfilment, her most precious experiences of life. Many fruits had been harvested which she would carry onwards. She would bring them again as soul faculties, capacities to be used next time.[2] What an enormous treasure house life on earth can be! She came more and more to understand its unique value, and was eager to prepare herself for her next encounter. But first there was a long way to go. Eventually she saw her newborn infant self once more, and the backwards journey through her entire previous life was complete.

Now a much more expansive sphere opened to her. She journeyed ever onwards, and stars began to reveal their scripted message. She felt herself being carried on invisible wings to another sphere. It was as though the radiance of the sun enfolded and warmed her.[3] She felt strangely at home within its orb of light. Here she recognized many fellow journeymen, those with whom she had travelled on earth. They celebrated her safe arrival.

The journey led her and others still further onwards. Many-coloured hues of wisdom shone upon her; and then a stronger force drew her on to what seemed the furthest outreach of time and memory. Beyond that she sensed there were no further time cycles, no connection whatever with anything she had known on earth. Here was 'Being' only. The great cosmic ritual which expressed itself on earth in rhythms and cycles, had no place here.

She ventured forth into the Beyond, tentatively at first, knowing that entrance to these exalted realms was only for those able to express on earth the aims and intentions of the divine.[4] But she also knew that she had riches to offer, many gifts to fertilize the purposes of these lofty regions; and so she stepped more courageously, garnering and giving as she was able.

Many of her friends remained in the Saturn sphere. There preparation could be made for a future life on earth; and as the great cosmic clock chimed the midnight hour, she also began to feel an intense longing for a new earthly life. The prospect filled her with elation. She must make preparations, for there was much to be done.

She set to work with purpose, building an imaginative picture of her next body, making it an image of what she would require on earth to fulfil her next task, to work further on her karma. Under the guidance of celestial powers, she chose her next parents, those able to give her the type of body she needed. She would have opportunity to work on it, refining details as its cells continually changed. She thought it likely that she would have a male body next time, one that would enable her soul to balance what had been gained as mother.

As she journeyed back towards the earth, she gathered forces from the planets, and built a body to house her soul on earth. And living solar forces provided ethereal substance to enliven the atoms of the body which her future parents would provide.[5] Finally, she gathered up her parcel of karma which she had deposited as she set forth on her travels, at the end of her previous life. It contained both treasures and burdens. All the resources of her soul would be needed to sort things out in her next life. For this she now felt better equipped than previously.

Mother-grandmother had travelled far. Was it for years or for centuries that she had journeyed beyond the confines of earth existence? Life on earth would be different this time, humanity more evolved in consciousness, and the earth itself greatly changed. She sensed impending dangers, and knew that tremendous challenges lay ahead. Yet she felt serenely confident as she waited.

She placed her being in the arms of the Infinite, and rejoiced.

# Postscript

## Mother and the Pursuit of Happiness

In fairytales we learn that the handsome Prince and the beautiful Princess were married and lived happily ever after. Theirs was a state of continuing bliss.

Today, this state of happiness is sought differently. There are a variety of meditative practices aimed at transcending the dullness of the mundane and reaching a state of euphoric bliss; there are drugs to carry the soul into states of ecstasy. In such a scenario the drug becomes the handsome Prince, and far from wooing the Princess, relentlessly carries her off into strange uncharted realms. The honeymoon becomes a trip full of tumultuous passions, and happiness quickly flies out of the casement window. Then there is the 'corporate world' described by Jan (see Chapter 4) where happiness is sought by abandoning the self and immersing one's soul in the grind of ongoing activities, a kind of 'perpetuum mobile' where the Princess eventually withers and emptiness ensues.

So why is a state of happiness so elusive for many people today?

*Happiness will never be achieved by actively seeking it,* for it is not a thing in itself. It cannot be 'found'. It is a by-product, and its 'producer' is PURPOSE. The purposeful life can give rise to happiness; but, having recognised and undertaken a purposeful task, the soul can rest content in itself. Then it becomes irrelevant whether one is happy or not. To be engaged in purposeful work is, itself, enough.

In mothering, the child becomes the purpose of the mother. She expresses her purpose by establishing family life and by meeting the needs of the child. As the years go by she is able to reflect on her purpose. When she recognises herself as the Divine Mother made manifest, when, with the Father she creates the Son and offers her Creation to the world, it is then that she is able to experience the Divine Purpose. The experiences of purposeful daily life give rise to the possibility of happiness.

# Appendix A
# Homogenised Milk

Studies have shown that there are more deaths from myocardial infarction (MI) amongst people who drink milk than amongst those who do not. At Fairfield University (USA), Dr Kurt Osler has explained why. The problem is not with milk, per se, but with homogenised milk. The cow, in creating the milk, loads it with a highly oxidising enzyme, zanthine oxidase. This enzyme is normally in large particles, too large to pass through the intestinal lining of a person drinking the milk. In the process of homogenising milk, however, these large enzyme particles are broken into very small particles, which can pass through the intestinal lining into the bloodstream, where they do a lot of damage to the blood vessels. Cheese, which is not made from homogenised milk, is shown not to increase the incidence of MI deaths. Skim milk is produced from homogenised milk and is therefore also implicated in MI deaths.

The above article was published in June 1993 in the newsletter of the International Association of Cancer Victors and Friends, Melbourne, Australia. I wish to acknowledge the kind permission of the editor, given verbally, to reprint it here. J.S.

# Appendix B
# How to make Almond milk

Blanch 1/2 cup of almonds by soaking for about ten minutes in boiling water, and then removing skins.

Soak blanched almonds in a cup of cold water for half an hour. Grind nuts to a fine pulp in a mortar and pestle, and gradually add the water in which they have been soaked; or water and nuts can be mixed together in a blender.

Then strain off the milk through cheesecloth, squeezing firmly. If possible, use biodynamically grown almonds. The pulp can be used in a variety of ways -- for example, blend with a soft cheese to make a spread, add to yogurt or whatever else you may like.

It is helpful to make a small bag for straining purposes, either from cheesecloth or a very fine muslin.

# Appendix C
# Rice

For many hundreds of years, rice has been a staple food for people of eastern countries; and these people have always been known for their dedication to the spiritual rather than to the earthly. This has been so from time immemorial, especially for Indian people. They expressed this attitude by declaring that the earth is maya (illusion), and the only reality is spirit. In the Bhagavad Gita, Krishna expresses this clearly. He tells Arjuna, who represents a thoughtful seeking soul, 'That which is unreal hath no shadow of Real Being, notwithstanding the illusion of appearance ...'[1]

When we consider the nature of rice, we gain an understanding of how this attitude has endured over so many hundreds of years. For rice could be described as a non-earthly food. It has its roots in paddy fields, the watery element, rather than the earthly. Is it any wonder then, that ancient Indian religion and philosophy considered the earth to be illusion?

At a superficial level, rice may therefore be considered the ideal introductory food for an infant; and from the point of view of digestibility it places no strain on the immature digestive system. Baby rice is an established product recommended as an early addition to the baby's diet

But in the book, *The Incarnating Child*, the infant is described as an incarnating human spirit; that is, a human being seeking incarnation on earth, wanting to gain a consciousness of the earthly. If this is taken seriously and brought to bear on practical issues such as the infant's food, it raises questions as to the suitability of rice being given in the early months, often as a first food. This would seem to have the very opposite effect to the one the child is seeking, and could be a hindrance rather than a help for coming to terms with life on earth. In the above book it was stated that:

..the child's diet must be such that there will be a co-ordination between bodily needs and the needs of the spirit; body growth and the incarnation process must work hand-in-hand.

This must be a guiding principle in introducing food to the infant. From this point of view, rice should not be given as an introductory food. The ideal time to add it to the baby's diet is after the child has first been 'grounded' by having root vegetables; that is, at approximately eight months of age. Then rice is an excellent food, and may help to balance the strong earthly forces, expressed in materialism, that are so prevalent today.

From this we can gather that our theme of mothering places a responsibility on mother not only to see the child as an incarnating human spirit, but also to apply this knowledge to all the most practical aspects of the child's care.

1   *Bhagavad Gita,* translated by Yogi Ramacharaka. Part 2, 'The Inner Doctrine. The Yogi Publication Society, USA, 1935

# Chapter Notes

## Introduction

1  Rudolf Steiner was born in Austria in 1861. From childhood onwards he was aware of a dimension of life not perceptible to bodily senses. This can be called 'the spiritual world'. As an adult, he sought to understand the relationship between this and the natural world. In his search he came to recognize the significance of thinking for spiritual investigation as well as for natural scientific research. He was thus able to explore both worlds with equal objectivity and precision. He presented in books and lectures the body of knowledge he thus obtained, couching it in thought forms suitable for today's consciousness.

2  Joan Salter: *The Incarnating Child*, chapter 13: 'The Madonna's Cloak'. Hawthorn Press, Stroud, UK, 1987.

## Prologue

1  Rudolf Steiner: *Between Death and Rebirth*, Berlin 1912-13, Rudolf Steiner Press, London, 1975.

2  Geoffrey Hodson: *The Miracle of Birth*, The Theosophical Publishing House Ltd, London 1929.

3  See Jane's birth experience, chapter 2.

4  Geoffrey Hodson: *The Miracle of Birth*, op. cit.

5  Rudolf Steiner gave very many lectures on reincarnation and karma. These have been published in a number of books, such as *Manifestations of Karma*, Rudolf Steiner Press, London 1968; *Reincarnation and Karma*, Steiner Book Centre Inc., North Vancouver, Canada 1977; and *Theosophy*, Anthroposophic Press Inc., New York.

# Chapter 1

1 Dr Thomas Verney with John Kelly: *The Secret Life of the Unborn Child*, Warner Books, UK, 1993.
2 Rudolf Steiner: *The Fall of the Spirits of Darkness*, lecture 4. Rudolf Steiner Press, London, 1993.
3 Geoffrey Hodson: *The Miracle of Birth*, chapter 9.
4 Karl König: *Penguins, Seals, Dolphins, Salmon and Eels*, Floris Books, Scotland, 1984.
5 Ibid.
6 Fred Bruemmer and Brian Davies: *Seasons of the Seal*, Northwood Press Inc., Wisconsin, USA, 1988.

# Chapter 2

1 I will alternate male/female forms from chapter to chapter, to avoid the awkwardness of saying him/her each time – Joan Salter.
2 A type of breathing taught in yoga. This technique slows down the breathing, which in turn slows the heart beat, altering brain-wave patterns and calming the nervous system.
3 Early in the 18th century the Amish people settled in Pennsylvania, USA. Since that time their lifestyle has not altered, and they reject much that we take for granted, e.g. telephones, electricity, cars, etc. Most of them are farmers who lead a quiet and simple life. Their birthing practices could be described as 'natural'.
4 *The Four Seasons and the Archangels*. Five lectures given by Rudolf Steiner in Dornach, Switzerland, 5th to 13th October, 1923. Lecture 2, 'The Christmas Imagination'. Rudolf Steiner Press, London 1984. Cheryl advises that 'it is necessary to read the whole book to gain a context for these thoughts'.

# Chapter 3

1 This section is based on lecture 4 of a series given by Father Bede Griffiths, entitled *This World and the Absolute Reality.* The series is available in tape form.
2 Robert Graves: *The Greek Myths,* volume 1. Pelican Books, Middlesex, UK, 1955.
3 Ibid.
4 This section is based on the book *The Great Initiates* by Edouard Schuré, chapters 30-34. Rudolf Steiner Publications Inc., New York 1961.
5 Isidore Epstein: *Judaism.* Pelican Books, Middlesex, UK, 1959.
6 Dante Alighieri: *The Divine Comedy 1: Hell,* translated by Dorothy L. Sayers. Penguin Classics, Middlesex, UK, 1949.
7 Johann Wolfgang von Goethe: *Faust, part 11, Act 1.* Translated by Philip Wayne, Penguin Classics, London 1959.
8 Ibid, Act 5.
9 Ecclesiastes, chapter 7, v. 25; chapter 8, vs. 9 and 16.
10 W. Sucher: *Cosmic Christianity, an Outline,* Astrosophy Research Center, Meadow Vista, Ca 95722, USA 1982.

# Chapter 4

1 The 'Vital Years' seminar is held biannually in capital cities in Australia, and is a forum for Steiner kindergarten teachers. The 1995 seminar was held in Melbourne, Victoria.
2 A private practice in maternal and child care founded by Joan Salter in 1976. It is concerned with the child's upbringing in the home and is based on Rudolf Steiner's outline of the human being.
3 Melinda has asked that what she actually wrote in this sentence be included. It is 'Hearing you speak with such authority and wisdom about what I and other mothers do...' In the book I have deleted the latter phrase, because I do not regard myself as having either of these qualities!

# Chapter 5

1 From an article written by Dr Desmond Gurry, published in *Focus* – 'Patient Management', May 1989. Dr Desmond Gurry is Senior Lecturer in Paediatrics at the University of Western Australia, and Consultant Physician at Princess Margaret Hospital for Children, Perth, Western Australia.

2 Cf *Breast Feeding Matters* by Maureen Minchin, chapter 1. Alma Publications and George Allen & Unwin, Australia 1985.

3 I am in touch with this generation of women. They are now grandmothers, some of whom often come to the Gabriel Centre when their daughter attends with her child. A number of them now regret that they did not persevere with breastfeeding in spite of being told that it didn't really matter. All of the ones I have spoken to *felt* that breastfeeding was the best.

4 Figures from Hambraeus.

5 From *Dairy Science Abstracts,* vol. 32, 1970 (with the exception of 'donkey').

6 Bruce L. Larson and Vearl P. Smith (ed.): *Lactation: a comprehensive treatise,* vol. 3, 1974.

7 Hermann Poppelbaum: *Man and Animal. Their Essential Difference.* Anthroposophical Publishing Co., London 1960.

8 Cf Rudolf Steiner: *Occult Science – an Outline,* chapter 4. Rudolf Steiner Press, London 1962/3.

9 Victor Bott: *Anthroposophical Medicine,* chapter 13. Rudolf Steiner Press, London 1978.

10 Ibid.

11 In an article published in *Natural Food and Farming Magazine,* USA.

12 Johann Wolfgang von Goethe: *Faust,* Part 1. Translated by Philip Warne, Penguin Classics, London 1949.

13 Rudolf Steiner: *The Etherisation of the Blood,* lecture of 1.10.1911. Rudolf Steiner Press, London, 1953.

14 See chapter 4.

15 This Foundation Stone was laid in September 1913. The Goetheanum is a world centre for the work of Rudolf Steiner.

The first building was destroyed by fire on 31 December 1922. A second building now stands in its place.

# Chapter 6

1   In the article cited in chapter 5 (Note 1), Dr Gurry quotes from a speech given by Dr G Kneebone at a Symposium 'Current trends in infant nutrition', Sydney 1985. He says, 'Kneebone has described how knowledge (of bottle feeding) has been acquired through a series of catastrophes in infant feeding.'
2   Joan Salter: *The Incarnating Child,* Hawthorn Press, UK, 1987. See appendices.
3   Rudolf Steiner: *Theosophy,* chapter 1, section 4. Anthroposophic Press Inc., New York 1971.
4   See chapter 5, note 1.
5   This information was given to me by verbal communication only.
6   Ibid.
7   Cf an article in *Family Doctor,* 21 July 1995.
8   Rudolf Hauschka: *Nutrition,* Stuart and Watkins, London 1967. This book contains an Addendum by Grethe Hauschka MD, which has a section on nutrition in childhood and youth.

# Chapter 7

1   The content of this chapter is based on a lecture given by Leanne Moraes to a group of kindergarten parents in Geelong, Victoria, some years ago. I am grateful for permission to use it.

# Chapter 8

1   Alfred Tennyson: *Morte d'Arthur.*
2   Rudolf Steiner: *Preparing for the Sixth Epoch,* The Anthroposophic Press Inc., New York 1976.
3   This is clearly portrayed in *Exodus.*

4   See note 2 above.
5   Joan Salter: *The Incarnating Child,* chapter 13. Hawthorn Press, UK, 1987.
6   Cf Rudolf Meyer: *Rhythms in Human Beings and the Cosmos,* Floris Books, Scotland, 1985.
7   Tine Thevenin: *The Family Bed.* Avery Publishing Group Inc., New Jersey, USA, 1987.
    See also: Aletha J Solter: *The Aware Baby,* chapter 3. Shining Star Press, Goleta, California, USA 1994.
8   Rudolf Steiner: *Theosophy,* chapter 1.
9   Marshall H. Klaus and John H. Kennell: *Maternal-Infant Bonding.* The CV Mosby Company, St Louis, USA, 1976.
10  Ibid, chapter 1.
11  Ibid, chapter 3.
12  See note 2.

# Chapter 9

1   *Genesis,* chapters 1 and 2.
2   *The Revelation of Saint John the Divine,* chapter 21.
3   *Genesis,* chapter 1, v. 27. The 'them' in this verse refers to the primal human being created 'in the image of God'. Cf also: Rudolf Steiner: *Cosmic Memory,* chapter 6. New York 1971.

# Chapter 10

1   From age 21-28 the ego penetrates and learns to use what Rudolf Steiner calls the 'Sentient Soul'. *The Incarnating Child,* by Joan Salter, calls this the Experiencing Principle of the soul (see Chapter 15). This soul principle includes the feeling life; and during pregnancy, particularly the later months, and the early childhood years, it is this which is greatly intensified in the mother. An understanding of the unfolding of the human soul can be gained by self observation and by observation of, and conversations with others.
2   Penelope Leach: *Children First,* The Penguin Group, London 1994.

3   Steve Biddulph: *More Secrets of Happy Children*, Bay Books, Sydney, 1994.

4   Rudolf Steiner has outlined the development of the child in an essay entitled *The Education of the Child in the Light of Anthroposophy*, Rudolf Steiner Press, London 1965.

5   Cf A.C.Harwood: *The Way of a Child*, Rudolf Steiner Press, London 1940.

6   *Ecclesiastes*, chapter 3.

7   Joseph Chilton Pearce: *The Magical Child*, chapter 13. Bantam Books, 1977.

8   Ibid.

9   Perhaps from a soul point of view, age three would be more accurate. It is then that the child is freed from the mother's 'soul body'.

10  *The Magical Child*, chapter 11.

11  In *The Incarnating Child* by Joan Salter, this is referred to as the 'folding back of the Madonna's cloak'.

12  See Rudolf Steiner: *Cosmic Memory*, chapter 6. ('In itself the soul is two-sided: male-female.') See chapter 12.

# Chapter 11

1   An Australian literary magazine. The article was published in no. 323, vol. XL, no. 1-2.

# Chapter 12

1   I wish to acknowledge my debt and gratitude to Erwin Berney, from whom I gained some of the ideas which led to this chapter. J.S.

2   Emil Bock was a priest of the Christian Community and one of its founding members. He was born in Wuppertal, Germany, in 1895, and died in 1959.

3   Emil Bock: *Genesis: Creation and the Patriarchs*, Floris Books, Scotland, 1983.

4   See Rudolf Steiner: *The Manifestations of Karma*, lecture 10. Rudolf Steiner Press, London 1968.

5 See Rudolf Steiner: *Occult Science – an Outline*, chapter 6. This chapter is entitled: 'Present and Future Evolution of the World and Mankind'.
6 Ibid, chapter 4: 'For whatever is to emerge at a certain time in human evolution will always be slowly maturing in the preceding time'.
7 F. Max Müller: *The Science of Language*, Longmans Green and Co., London, 1885.
8 Ibid.
9 Andrew Welburn: *The Beginnings of Christianity*, Floris Books, Edinburgh, 1991.

# Chapter 13

1 I have known a number of mothers who have wept after bidding their child 'goodbye' on the first day of school. This applies particularly to a first child.

# Chapter 14

1 This 'new power' which enters the soul at 35 was called by Steiner 'Bewusstseinseele'. (Cf *Theosophy*, chapter 1, Rudolf Steiner Press, London 1922.) It has been translated as 'consciousness soul' and 'spiritual soul'.
2 Cf Norbert Glas: *The Fulfilment of Old Age*, chapter 1. Anthroposophic Press Inc., New York 1970
3 Ibid.
4 Cf Rudolf Steiner: *Study of Man*, Rudolf Steiner Press, London, 1966. Lecture 7 of this series states: 'In middle age the human being is more predominantly soul, and in old age he is more spiritual. See also: Norbert Glas, op. cit., chapter 1.
5 Cf Norbert Glas: *The Fulfilment of Old Age*, chapter 1, op. cit.

# Chapter 15

1   For this chapter I have used Steiner's 4th Mystery Play, *The Soul's Awakening*, Scenes 5 and 6 (Steiner Book Centre, Toronto, Canada 1973); *Theosophy* by Rudolf Steiner, chapter 2 and Chapter 3, Section 4 (op.cit.); and *Between Death and Rebirth*, ten lectures given by Rudolf Steiner in Berlin 5th November 1912 to 1st April 1913. (Rudolf Steiner Press, London 1975).

2   Rudolf Steiner: *Theosophy*, chapter 2, op.cit.

3   Rudolf Steiner: *The Soul's Awakening*, scene 5, op.cit.

4   Rudolf Steiner: *Theosophy*, chapter 3, section 4, op.cit.

5   Rudolf Steiner: *Between Death and Rebirth*, lecture 10, op.cit.

# Bibliography

**Biddulph** Steve: *More Secrets of Happy Children*, Bay Books, Australia 1994

**Bock** Emil: *Genesis*, Floris Books, Scotland 1983. *The Apocalypse of St John*, Floris Books, Scotland 1957

**Bott** Victor: *Anthroposophical Medicine*, Rudolf Steiner Press, London 1978

**Bruemmer** Fred and **Davies** Brian: *Seasons of the Seal*, North Word Press Inc., USA 1988

**Chilton** Pearce Joseph: *The Magical Child*, Bantam Books, New York 1977

**Dante**: *The Divine Comedy*, Book 1 'Hell' and Book 3 'Paradise', translated by Dorothy Sayers, Penguin Classics, UK 1949

**Epstein** Isidore: *Judaism*, Penguin Books Ltd., UK 1959

**Glas** Norbert: *The Fulfilment of Old Age*, Anthroposophical Press Inc., New York 1970

**Goethe** Johann Wolfgang von: *Faust*, Part 2, translated by Philip Wayne, Penguin Classics, UK 1959

**Graves** Robert: *The Greek Myths* Book 1, Penguin Books Ltd., UK 1955

**Harwood** A.C.: *The Way of a Child*, Rudolf Steiner Press, London 1940

**Hauschka** Rudolf: *Nutrition*, Stuart and Watkins, London 1967

**Hodson** Geoffrey: *The Miracle of Birth*, The Theosophical Publishing House, London 1929

**Klaus** Marshall and **Kennell** John: *Maternal-infant bonding*, The C.V. Mosley Company, USA 1976

**Knisely** Kim Gehman: *A is for Amish*. Kniseley Stoltzfus Books, USA 1993

**König** Karl: *Embryology and World Evolution*. 2 lectures printed in the British Homoeopathic Journal, Vol LVIII, Jan. and April 1969; *Penguins, Seals, Dolphins, Salmon and Eels*, Floris Books, Scotland 1984

**Leach** Penelope: *Children First*, The Penguin Group, London 1994

**Meyer** Rudolf: *Rhythms in Human Beings and the Cosmos*, Floris Books, Scotland 1985

**Minchin** Maureen: *Breast Feeding Matters*, Alma Publications and George Allen & Unwin, Australia 1983

**Pfeiffer** Ehrenfried: *Heart Lectures*. 3 lectures given at Spring Valley, USA, Mercury Press, USA 1982

**Poppelbaum** Hermann: *Man and Animal*, Anthroposophical Publishing Company, London 1960

**Salter** Joan: *The Incarnating Child*, Hawthorn Press, UK 1987

**Schmidt** Gerhardt: *The Dynamics of Nutrition*, Proteus Verlag, Switzerland 1960

**Schuré** Edouard: *The Great Initiates*, Steiner Books, New York, second edition 1992

**Solter** Aletha J: *The Aware Baby*, Shining Star Press, Goleta, California, USA 1994

**Steiner** Rudolf: *The Soul's Awakening*, Steiner Book Centre, Canada 1973; *The Education of the Child*, Rudolf Steiner Press, London, 1965; *Occult Science*, Rudolf Steiner Press, London. George and Mary Adams translation 1962-63; *Cosmic Memory*, Rudolf Steiner Publications, New York 1971; *Theosophy*, Rudolf Steiner Press, London. Revised translation 1970; *The Etherisation of the Blood*. Lecture given in Basel, 1 October 1911. Rudolf Steiner Press, London 1971; *Prefacing the Sixth Epoch*. Lecture given in Dusseldorf, 15 June, 1915. Anthroposophical Press, USA 1951; *Genesis*. 10 lectures given in Munich, 17-26 August 1910. Anthroposophical Publishing Co., London 1959; *Isis Madonna*. Lecture given in Berlin, 29 April 1909, Mercury Press, USA 1987; *Between Death and Rebirth*. 10 lectures given in Berlin, 5 November 1912 to I April 1913, Rudolf Steiner Press, London 1975; *The Fall of the Spirits of Darkness*. 14 lectures give in Dornach, 29 September to 28 October 1917. Rudolf Steiner Press UK 1993; *Karmic Relationships*. A series of 80 lectures given in 1924. Rudolf Steiner Press in 8 volumes 1956.

**Sucher** Willi: *Cosmic Christianity*, Astrosophy Research Centre, USA 1982

**Thevenin** Tina: *The Family Bed*, Avery Publishing Group Inc., USA 1987

**Verney** Thomas with **Kelly** John: *The Secret Life of the Unborn Child,* Warner Books, London 1993
**Yogi** Ramacharaka (trans.): *Bhagavad Gita,* The Yogi Publication Society, 1935

# Further Recommended Reading

**Carey** Diana and **Large** Judy: *Festivals, Family and Food,* Hawthorn Press, Stroud, UK 1982
**Coplen** Dotty Turner: *Parenting - a path through Childhood.* Floris Books, Scotland 1982
**Davey** Gudrun and **Voors** Bon: *Lifeways,* Hawthorn Press, Stroud, UK 1983
**Drake** Stanley: *Path to Birth,* Floris Books, Scotland 1979
**Elkind** David: *The Hurried Child,* Addison-Wesley Publishing Company Inc., USA 1931
**Gibson** Margaret: *Becoming a mother,* Hale and Iremonger, Australia 1986
**Glas** Norbert: *Conception, Birth and Early Childhood.* Anthroposophic Press Inc., Spring Valley, USA 1972
**Griffiths** Bede: *The Marriage of East and West,* Fount Paperbacks, London 1982
**König** Karl: *Brothers and Sisters,* Anthroposophic Press Inc., Spring Valley, USA 1963
**Lievegoed** Bernhard: *Towards the 21st Century.* Lectures given in Spring Valley, USA 1965. Steiner Book Centre, Canada 1972
**Phillips** Virginia: *Successful Breast Feeding,* Nursing Mothers Association of Australia 1976
**Steiner** Rudolf: *The Evolution of Consciousness,* 13 lectures given in North Wales, UK., 19 to 31 August, 1923. Rudolf Steiner Press, London 1926; *At the Gates of Spiritual Science.* 14 lectures given in Stuttgart, 22 August to 4 September 1906, Rudolf Steiner Press, London 1970; *Reincarnation and Karma.* 5 lectures given in Berlin and Stuttgart, January to March 1912. Anthroposophical Publishing Company, London 1960; *The Manifestations of Karma.* 11 lectures given in Hamburg, 16 to 28 May 1910. Rudolf Steiner Press, London 1969

# Other books from Hawthorn Press

## The Incarnating Child
*Joan Salter*

*'Our birth is but a sleep and a forgetting';*
Joan Salter picks up on Wordsworth's theme
and follows the soul life of tiny babies into
childhood and adolescence. A specialist in
maternal and child care, she addresses
physical, spiritual and psychological development as well as environmental factors. This
book will be particularly valuable for those
embarking on parenthood for the first time.

210 x 135mm; 224pp; illustrations and
photographs; paperback; 1 869 890 04 3

## Between Form and Freedom
**A practical guide to the teenage years**
*Betty Staley*

Betty Staley offers a wealth of insights about teenagers, providing a
compassionate, intelligent and intuitive look into the minds of children
and adolescents. She explores the nature of adolescence and looks at
teenagers' needs in relation to family, friends, schools, love and the arts.
Issues concerning stress, depression, drug and alcohol abuse and eating
disorders are included.
210 x 135mm; 288pp; sewn limp bound; illustrations;  1 869 890 08 6

## Festivals, Family and Food
*Diana Carey and Judy Large.*

A ideal companion to *Festivals Together,* this explores those numerous
annual 'feast days' which children love celebrating. It was written in
response to children and busy parents asking, 'What can we do at
Christmas and Easter? What games can we play? What can we make?'
200 x 250mm; 216pp; paperback; colour cover; fully illustrated;
0 950 706 23 X

# Festivals Together
## A guide to multi-cultural celebration
*Sue Fitzjohn, Minda Weston, Judy Large*

This is a resource guide for celebration, and for observing special days according to traditions based on many cultures. It brings together the experience, sharing and activities of individuals from multi-faith communities all over the world – Buddhist, Christian, Hindu, Jewish, Muslim and Sikh. Its unifying thread is our need for meaning, for continuity and for joy.

200 x 250mm; 224pp; paperback; fully illustrated; 1 869 890 46 9

# Parenting for a Healthy Future
*Dotty T. Coplen*

Here is a commonsense approach to the challenging art of parenting; an offer of genuine support and guidance to encourage parents to believe in themselves and their children. Dotty Coplen helps parents gain a deeper understanding of parenting children from both a practical and holistic, spiritual perspective.

216 x 138mm; 126pp; paperback; 1 869 890 53 1

# Manhood
## An action plan for changing men's lives
*Steve Biddulph*

'Most men don't have a life'. So begins the most powerful, practical and honest book ever to be written about men and boys. Not about our problems – but about how we can find the joy and energy of being in a male body with a man's mind and spirit – about men's liberation.

Steve Biddulph is Australia's best known family therapist and parenting author. *The Times* calls him 'a mix of Billy Connolly and Dr Spock ... a publishing phenomenon'. Born in Yorkshire, he makes regular lecture tours to Britain.

210 x 135mm; 272pp; paperback; b/w photos; 1 869 890 99 X

## Lifeways Working with family questions
### *ed Gudrun Davy and Bons Voors*

*Lifeways* is about children, about family life and about being a parent.
But above all it is about freedom, and how the tension between family
life and personal fulfilment can be resolved.
150 x 210mm; 328pp; 0 950 706 24 8

## Soulways
### Development, Crises and Illnesses of the Soul
### *Rudolf Treichler*

*Soulways* offers insights into personal growth through the phases and
turning points of human life. A profound picture of child and adult
development is given, including the developmental needs, potentials
and questions of each stage. Drawing on his work as a psychiatrist,
Treichler also explores the developmental disorders of soul life –
addictions, neuroses, hysteria, anorexia and schizophrenia.
210 x 135mm; 320pp; paperback; 1 869 890 13 2

## Tapestries Weaving Life's Journey
### *Betty Staley*

*Tapestries* gives a moving and wise guide to women's life phases.
Drawing on original biographies of a wide variety of women, informed
by personal experience and by her understanding of anthroposophy,
Betty Staley offers a vivid account of life journeys. This book helps
readers reflect on their own lives and prepare for the next step in
weaving their own biographical tapestry.
216 x 138mm; 336pp; paperback; 1 869 890 15 9

## The Twelve Senses
### *Albert Soesman*

The author provides a lively look at the senses – not merely the normal
five senses, but twelve: touch, life, self-movement, balance, smell, taste,
vision, temperature, hearing, language, the conceptual and the ego senses.
210 x 135mm; 176pp; paperback; 1 869 890 22 1

## ORDERS
**If you have difficulties ordering *Hawthorn Press* books from
a bookshop, you can order direct from: Scottish Book Source
Distribution, 137 Dundee Street, Edinburgh, EH11 1BG
Tel. 0131 229 6800   Fax. 0131 229 9070**